Bach's St. Matthew *Passion*

A CLOSER LOOK

MAGNUM OPUS

Edited by Robert Levine

Magnum Opus is a series for anyone seeking a greater familiarity with the cornerstones of Western Classical music—operatic, choral, and symphonic. An erudite collection of passionate, down-to-earth, and authoritative books on the works and their creators, Magnum Opus will build into an indispensable resource for anyone's musical library.

Forthcoming:

Beethoven's Fifth and Seventh Symphonies, by David Hurwitz

Handel's Messiah, by Ben Finane

Brahms's Symphonies, by David Hurwitz

Bach's St. Matthew Passion

A CLOSER LOOK

Victor Lederer

continuum

NEW YORK • LONDON

2008

The Continuum International Publishing Group Inc
80 Maiden Lane, New York, NY 10038

The Continuum International Publishing Group Ltd
The Tower Building, 11 York Road, London SE1 7NX
www.continuumbooks.com

Library of Congress Cataloging-in-Publication Data

Lederer, Victor.
  Bach's St. Matthew Passion : a closer look / Victor Lederer.
     p. cm.—(Magnum opus)
  Includes bibliographical references.
  ISBN-13: 978-0-8264-2940-7 (pbk. : alk. paper)
  ISBN-10: 0-8264-2940-8 (pbk. : alk. paper) 1. Bach, Johann
Sebastian, 1685–1750. Matthew passion. 2. Passion music—Analysis,
appreciation. I. Title.
  ML410.B13L39 2008
  782.23—dc22
                                        2008028621

Printed in the United States of America

for Paul

Contents

Acknowledgments

THANKS ARE DUE first and foremost to Bob Levine, my friend and editor, for his patience when progress on what had looked like a straightforward project slowed to a crawl. Bach's dense masterwork refused to be hurried once I began to live with it; and a despair of capturing in words the immensity and countless glories of the piece descended. As usual, Bob helped me with everything from easy questions of form, more difficult ones about content, and encouragement when I wondered what I was doing in taking up a topic so colossal. While I know the *St. Matthew Passion* better for having listened to it dozens of times in the recent months, my sense of just starting to know the work is more acute now than when I began.

Thanks, too, to my friend and teacher Bernie Rose for his help with technical questions about Bach's score, and for his invaluable insights, as well. A conversation with my friend Sasha Katsman, a passionate devotee of Bach's music, on the size and composition of Bach's chorus proved timely and is much appreciated. Thanks and love to my children— now magnificent adults—Paul and Karen; and, as always, to my wife, Elaine.

Chapter 1

*B*ach and the St. Matthew Passion

ALMOST THREE HUNDRED YEARS after its composition, Johann Sebastian Bach's *St. Matthew Passion* stands as one of the unshakeable pillars of Western musical culture, revered by professional musicians and audiences alike.

This is not to imply that the massive work can be even remotely described as easy. Bach's music—dark, intense, and in an arcane musical language—speaks less readily than the suave, memorable melodies and thunderous choruses from Handel's equally great but more approachable and popular *Messiah*. Even dedicated admirers of Bach, not to mention novice listeners, find the *St. Matthew Passion* daunting, the vast score offering none of the buoyant pleasures of the *Brandenburg Concertos* or Bach's other, more familiar instrumental music. A typical hearing of the *St. Matthew Passion* demands three hours of the most serious attention. Nevertheless, although the *St. Matthew Passion* is perhaps the least likely candidate for "casual" listening, its lofty tone of comes though clearly, even to someone hearing it for the first time in imperfect circumstances. Each and every subsequent careful listening proves shockingly revealing of Bach's power, boldness, and profundity.

The seriousness of the *St. Matthew Passion* is hardly surprising, given the subject—the final week of the life of Jesus, from his anointing in Bethany to his burial, as told in chapters 26 and 27 of the Gospel according to Matthew. The text, by Christian Friedrich Henrici, consists of free verses of a meditational nature, traditional Lutheran chorales—essentially hymns, which Bach rewrote extensively—and the Biblical text. The *Passion* is not, and could therefore never be, a Handelian celebration of the coming of the Messiah; it is, rather, a harrowing musical dramatization of, and meditation on, the final suffering and death of the obscure, perhaps mythical Palestinian Jew whose story and teachings would transform the world, for better and worse.

Henrici, working under the curious *nom de plume* Picander, did an excellent job, but it seems clear that Bach had much to say about the text, and may have selected some of the chorale texts himself. In this he acted much as would two of the greatest composers who followed: Verdi and Wagner, the twin titans of late-nineteenth-century opera. Verdi was notorious for bullying the theatrically effective and dramatically true out of his librettists. Dispensing with literary collaborators altogether, Wagner wrote his own libretti, with uneven results, that were nevertheless well-suited to his revolutionary concepts.

The *St. Matthew Passion* is an oratorio—a work of faith—not an opera. But Bach, like countless artists, found the human drama of Jesus's betrayal, trial, and death essential to his artistic conception. The oratorio form offered him the freedom to apply the full resources of his dramatic imagination to the narrative portions. Bach paces the two long sections in which the *Passion* is cast like acts of an opera, with an acute sense of dramatic flow and contrast. The manner, moreover, in which the singers play the roles in this sacred drama—the Evangelist, Pilate, Peter, Judas, and Jesus himself, among others—is a theatrical device common to opera, oratorio, and this particular type of Passion setting, known as an "oratorio Passion."

Unable to employ all the conventions of operatic form, however, Bach uses other means to tie the long work together, opening his "opera," for example, with a massive choral movement to create a mood of somber exaltation; in place of the concerted finales of opera, Bach concludes the two big sections of the *Passion* with choruses of a scale and emotional weight similar to that of the opening chorus. As the most prominent musical landmarks in the *Passion*, these three immense movements serve to frame and support the entire work, and Bach used other nonoperatic structures, as well, some of liturgical origin.

The arias, which express the pain of the sinful but repentant soul appalled by the humiliation of the Savior, take a reflective tone. Always following an advancement of the story, they function like their operatic cousins, expressing a range of emotions that seems more limited than those in contemporary operas, but also more profound. Like Handel, Rameau, and other masters of Baroque opera, Bach employed the compositional aesthetic known as "affect" to express an intense, nameable emotion. But in writing the *St. Matthew Passion* Bach was also deeply influenced by Pietism, a protestant religious movement that flourished from the sixteenth through the eighteenth centuries.

Pietism, along with Jansenist Catholicism in France and the ecstatic Hasidic worship of Eastern European Jews, was one of several religious revivals sweeping Europe in the seventeenth and eighteenth centuries. All refocused worship on the unobstructed relationship between the individual worshipper and God. At a moment when the notion of the individual was blossoming, the powerful messages put forward by these radical reforms proved irresistible in spite of the vigorous, sometimes violent opposition of religious and secular establishments. Pietist theology, with its noble ideals and individualism, ultimately saturated the Lutheran church and other reformed sects. Its effects can still be felt in the missionary fervor of many Lutheran congregations.

Other binding structural elements of the *Passion* include the chorales, and the keys—the tonalities—that Bach uses to link and contrast the various sections. All these elements that Bach skillfully assembles with his incomparable technique—his ability to make contrapuntal music expressive of profound thought and emotions—result in a work of overwhelming force. The dramatic structure and power of the *St. Matthew Passion* are obvious to anyone who has listened well to the work even once.

⌒

The conservative era and setting of Bach's birth and career prevented him from composing operas, or at least works so named; opera was forbidden in the pious Lutheran central German principalities of Thuringia where Bach was born, though it was permitted in neighboring Catholic Saxony where he spent most of his working life and died. Bach's more worldly contemporary Handel absorbed Italian music in Italy before finally settling in England, where he achieved renown as a master of Italian operas, then oratorios. Though composed to English texts, the latter have much in common musically with the operatic works they followed. Bach never traveled more than a few hundred miles from his birthplace, but his voracious musical intellect absorbed everything available to it, past and present. Bach clearly knew well the operatic traditions, already considerable by the eigheenth century, of Italy and its musical colony Austria, as well as the highly evolved musical and operatic traditions of France.

Baroque operas were viewed indulgently in the nine-teenth and early twentieth centuries as quaint and primitive ancestors of the modern opera as initiated by Mozart, to be brought to the ultimate heights of dramatic truth, in a supposed musical Darwinism, by the operatic masters who followed. Some cracks in this position appeared in the 1920s, when performers began to revive and find the merits of the operas of the indisputably admirable Handel. By the late twentieth century, the canon had expanded exponentially to include the works of Lully, Rameau, Purcell, and Alessandro Scarlatti, extending back to the three surviving operas by the mighty Claudio Monteverdi, one of the first operatic masters and still one of the greatest. The folly of denigrating compos-ers of such stature was soon devastatingly obvious; listening to their works is a matter of retuning our ears, which are accustomed to later vocal and orchestral styles that may be bigger but cannot sensibly be regarded as better.

Relatively few opera lovers, however, listen to musi-cal dramas before Mozart's, highly evolved though they now admit the early works to be. Most, accustomed to the high-flown melodies and forms of the favorites of the late Romantic and early modern eras, have difficulty with the closed forms and more restrained emotional expression of the Baroque opera. In these works, action rarely takes place on stage; nearly everything is related anecdotally in recitative; arias express the characters' emotions about the events as narrated. As an example, the William Christie/ Renée Fleming recording of the first act of Handel's three-act *Alcina* (1735) lasts fifty-eight minutes, of which the opening overture occupies six minutes. The act is broken into fourteen short scenes, with nine arias for the principal singers. There is a two-and-a-half minute chorus in scene 2. The arias take up just under forty-one minutes, thus carrying almost the entire weight of the work; those in act 1 of *Alcina* express tenderness, fond remembrance, despair, scorn, and more.

Arias in Baroque opera, typically in a three-part form known as *da capo*, though seemingly modest when compared to Wagner's or Donizetti's, are nevertheless nobly expressive of the single potent emotion each portrays. (Fewer people would fear opera if they understood that its goal is nothing more or less than the expression of the emotions that rule our lives.) This is the "affect," the specific passion—rage, madness, love, or hopelessness—contained in every aria of the age, an approach that would carry the weight of the operatic form well into the nineteenth century, when ensembles and continuous form replaced individual numbers. But whether in fixed form or embedded into the flow of the drama, arias continued to be vehicles for the intense expression of a single emotion long after the end of the Baroque era.

So potent is the drama of the *St. Matthew Passion* that one might almost forget its religious purpose and liturgical roots. But the Passion as a form is nearly as old as Christianity itself. As early as the fourth century, the story of Jesus' death was recited dramatically and partially sung during Holy Week services. By the Middle Ages, the Passion had settled on several conventions Bach himself would honor: the Evangelist was sung by a tenor, and Christ by a bass. The crowd, the portrayal of which would be crucial to the power of Bach's conception, was covered, curiously, by a single alto. In the fifteenth century, the Passion settings were chanted by three priests, perhaps to distinguish the characters from each other.

Martin Luther was a brilliant, complex man both of and ahead of his time. A talented musician, the Reformation's first leader wrote the texts to many famous Lutheran chorales. By translating the Bible into German, and envisioning the greater church—the community of sincere Christians—as "the universal priesthood of all believers,"[1] he also wrested Western Christian practice from the hands of the Catholic Church, granting freedom in modes of belief, practice, and litany to the reformed congregations of Germany. In this way, Luther took a major step toward establishing the subsequent religious emphasis on the direct relationship of the individual with God. A musical setting of the *St. Matthew Passion* by Luther's friend Johann Walther appeared in the 1520s, with the narrative portions in plainchant, which would have sounded much like what we know as Gregorian chant, and the cries of the mob rendered more realistically by four voices.

---

1. John B. Noss, *Man's Religions*, p. 485.

By the seventeenth century, the narrative form of the Passion, with its focus on the suffering of Jesus the man, had become chiefly, if not exclusively, a Protestant form of musical worship. The services—masses, matins, and vespers—with their prayers and frequent reminders of the mediating role of the Catholic Church itself, abandoned by reformed groups, naturally remained the glorious musical property of that older faith. Though staunchly Lutheran himself, Bach's settings of the Mass—including his stupendous Mass in B minor—reflect the intimate proximity of Catholics and Protestants in the central German principalities, his patron, the Elector of Saxony, being Catholic.

Three Passion settings (Luke, John, and Matthew) are attributed to Heinrich Schütz, Bach's greatest German predecessor. They are what is known as "responsorial" Passions; the opening and closing sections, as well as the parts of the crowds, the High Priests, and the Disciples are sung by small vocal ensembles, while the narrative and the role of Jesus is sung by a single voice, usually a bass. Bach's two surviving Passions sound positively Wagnerian in comparison to Schütz's stark settings for voices only, which make for challenging listening today.

Schütz was deeply influenced, just as Bach would be, by Italian music, the dominant European musical culture of the age. As a young man, Schütz studied and became close friends with the brilliant Venetian composer Giovanni Gabrieli. In 1628, Schütz returned to Italy to study with Claudio Monteverdi, where he fell for the rest of his long life under the spell of that mold-shattering founder of Baroque style. Thanks to Schütz's fluency in the Italian compositional manner, much of his devotional music sounds as though it were composed by Monteverdi or another of his followers. Far more congenial than the German Passions, and closer in spirit to Bach's devotional works as well, are Schütz's Passion-like oratorio settings of other Biblical texts in the Italian manner, which betray their composer's origins and Lutheran faith through their German language alone. The *Sacred Symphonies* and *Little Sacred Concerti*, not to mention the longer oratorios, *The History of the Resurrection of Jesus Christ* (ca. 1623), *The Seven Words of Christ on the Cross* (1645), and above all, the wonderful *Christmas Story* (1660), employ Biblical text in musical declamation modeled directly on the intensely expressive recitatives and affect-laden arias of Monteverdi and others, interspersed with choral movements.

Schütz learned from Monteverdi how to set sacred texts to broad choral or solo melodies over powerful dance rhythms. The friction between long, chantlike melodies setting a devotional text over the irresistible and very secular rhythm of the dance is a primary source of the nerve-wracking expressive power of Monteverdi's *Vespers of 1610* (which, like Bach's B-minor Mass, stands as one of the landmarks of choral music composed apparently without commission or expectation of performance.) In his own choral masterworks written in the Italian mode, Schütz also exploits the tensions inherent in this conflict of sacred and secular styles with devastating skill.

The same driving energy in Bach's music—which seems rarely if ever to depart from the rhythms of dance—also expresses the sacred through worldly means. Over and over his devotional music (and of course his instrumental music) dances with joy, or moves, as in the *St. Matthew Passion*, to the more solemn choreography of slow courtly dances like the allemande and the sarabande. In the smooth, floating, almost arhythmic polyphony of the masses and motets by Giovanni da Palestrina, we seem to hear the language of heaven itself. But the passionately declaimed operatic melodies and surging rhythms employed by Monteverdi, Schütz, Handel, and Bach speak with the accents and rhythms of our own visceral lives, evoking the tension between universal carnal impulses and higher consciousness that lies at the very foundation of human existence.

Schutz's Passions for unaccompanied voices honored a Lutheran tradition forbidding instrumental music in church during Holy Week, formerly the only time of year these works were performed. But this old-fashioned approach to the Passion was not the only path for German composers of the seventeenth century; lesser-known composers, including Thomas Strotius, Thomas Selle, and Johann Sebastiani, working for more liberal courts and congregations, ignored the old rules. In addition to orchestrating his *St. John Passion* lavishly, Selle composed as its conclusion a chorus based on the well-known chorale "O Lamm Gottes unschuldig" (O innocent Lamb of God), which Bach would later weave into the opening movement of the *St. Matthew Passion*. In his own *St. Matthew Passion* of 1672, Sebastiani gave the words sung by Jesus a "halo" of calm strings that is one of the most striking aspects of Bach's version.[2]

Composers of Bach's generation, working with Pietistic libretti, added to the structure of the Passion oratorio the contemplative arias that are among the best-loved portions

---

2. William Mann, "Bach's St. Matthew Passion: The Passion Story in Music," p. 2.

of Bach's Passions. Reinhard Keiser composed in 1717 a *St. Mark Passion* that was widely admired and served as a model for other composers, most likely including Bach. Keiser, who worked in Hamburg, also composed more than one hundred operas. The 1721 St. *Mark Passion* of Johann Kuhnau, Bach's predecessor as cantor in Leipzig, ends with a sorrowful choral lullaby over the entombed Jesus, as do Bach's Passions. The attribution to Handel of the so-called *Brockes Passion* (named for the librettist) is now considered doubtful.

Opera and Pietism had both added powerful personal emotions to the form by the time Bach began to write his Passion settings. It sounds incredible and amusing to listeners now that Bach was warned by the elders of St. Thomas Church in conservative Leipzig not to make his cantatas and Passions "too operatic," but so he was. The conflict between Pietist and traditional Lutheran theologies are irrelevant today, but the oratorios of Bach and Handel, both rich in meditative and dramatic expressivity and power, reach across the centuries with ease.

Bach, of course, was a devout Lutheran at a time when that faith was experiencing profound changes from within. The Pietist movement, a reformation within this reformed church, was changing the manner of Lutheran worship. The effect of Pietism on Bach's life and religious music is immeasurable. The texts of his church cantatas and the two surviving Passions, strongly Pietist in spirit, are full of meditative intensity and high-strung, often morbid imagery—not unlike many opera libretti. These texts stimulated Bach's ready imagination to some of its greatest peaks. The tortured intricacy of Bach's melodies, as they restlessly rise, fall, turn, twist, break, stop, then struggle back into motion, reflect the composer's obsessive need to capture the slightest nuance of meaning of every word he set. As Leo Schrade, in his short but fine study *Bach: The Conflict between the Sacred and the Secular*, observes:

> Bach did not allow Pietism to make itself much felt in his external life. But he admitted that it exerted its influence upon his religious ideas of art. And here, indeed, Pietism was of far-reaching consequence. For the Pietist religious intensity came from his attitude toward the evangelical word of the Bible; he discarded the dogmatic meaning which tradition had honored. He devoted himself to the direct meaning of the word. He believed that intimate and spiritual conversation with God will reveal the true and pious sense of the word. He must endeavor to exhaust the inherent secrets of the word in order to find God through it.[3]

Early Lutheran hymns, sung by the congregations, use the German plural pronouns *wir* (we) and *unser* (our), meaning "we, the congregation" implicitly embracing the wider community of believers as well. A number of the old chorales Bach used in the *St. Matthew Passion* employ the first-person plural, including the three crucial choruses that are the work's main landmarks. These pronouns represent an immense, unbridgeable split with the Roman Catholic liturgy, effectively demoting the priest-celebrant from his lead role in the drama of the Mass. With this, the role of the church itself, with all its dogma and hierarchies, was also questioned and ultimately reduced. Another massive shift in the practice of Christian worship brought about by Luther

---

3. Leo Schrade, *Bach: The Conflict between the Sacred and the Secular*, pp. 53–54.

and his followers was to hold the service in the vernacular, so that it might be understood rather than veiled in the mystery of Latin.

Bach and his librettists for the Passions and the cantatas took matters a step further, emphasizing Pietistic belief in the individual's direct connection, through prayer and meditation, to God. Henrici's lyrics for every aria but one in the *St. Matthew Passion* are in first-person singular: the singer, representing the human soul, sinful by nature but strong in faith, sings as *ich*—I. The *St. John Passion* of three years earlier presents a similar pattern, as do many of the surviving church cantatas. What Bach and his librettists (including one female writer) sought to portray was the soul reflecting with feeling on an aspect of God, be it the terrible suffering of Jesus, or on his mercy, or on the divine glory.

A more curious aspect of Pietist literary meditations can be found in their morbid and obsessive emphasis on the details of Jesus's suffering. Consider, for example, the title and guilt-ridden text of Bach's cantata *Mein Herze schwimmt im Blut* (My Heart Swims in Blood), or these lyrics from an aria and recitative from the cantata *Jesu, der du meine Seele* (Jesus, you who my soul), first performed in 1724:

> Thy blood, which cancels my guilt
> Makes my heart feel light again . . .

> The wounds, the nails, the crown and the grave,
> The blows that were dealt the Savior there
> Are from henceforth signs of triumph
> And can endow me with new strength. . . .

These are matched by the commitments of the singers, representing the soul:

> Though all hell should call me to the fight
>
> Jesus will stand beside me
>
> That I may take heart and win the day.

And:

> This my heart, marked with the grief
>
> Which Thy precious blood did scatter,
>
> Which was shed upon the cross,
>
> I give to thee, Lord Jesus Christ.[4]

This is much the same kind of language Henrici provided for Bach in his text for the *St. Matthew Passion*. The words *blood, tears, weeping, suffering, distress, mourning, bitter,* and, above all, *heart,* and their variants, dominate the non-Biblical sections—the arias, chorales, and some recitatives—to an astonishing degree. A modern, secular listener following the text may well perceive the narrow verbal range of Henrici's libretto as odd, and his imagery as gruesome, but this is how Pietist writers expressed themselves. It is, moreover, just the sort of figurative devotional language Bach understood and wanted to set; the relentless focus of Henrici's libretto allowed the composer to write music of a fearful intensity.

Another feature of Henrici's style is the use of contrast, irony, and paradox to remind the listener or worshipper of the generosity of a God who would send his son to Earth as a man, then sacrifice him for the miserable, sinning race of men. Again and again, Henrici recalls Jesus's *love* and

---

4. Translated by Gudrun Meier.

graciousness, faithfulness, righteousness, trustiness, sinlessness, and *his merciful will.* In more elaborate metaphors, Jesus is referred to as *husband to the women of Zion* (itself a metaphor for the community of worshippers), *guardian, conqueror, lord of vassals* (in the feudal sense), *shepherd, lamb, fount of nourishment,* and *precious keepsake.*

Bach composed about three hundred cantatas, chiefly on sacred subjects, with some remarkable forays into the secular, over the course of his working life; of these, about one-third have been lost. In the surviving works in this category, Bach practiced his art at his usual high level, covering an immense range of musical styles. Their emotional range far exceeds those of the *Passions,* which may be more profound, but are necessarily narrower.

A somber, Pietistic cantata like *Jesu, der du meine Seele* sounds as though it might have been lifted directly from one of the Passions. But others, such as *Wachet auf, ruft uns die Stimme* ("Awaken," calls the voice to us) or *Herz und Mund und Tat und Leben* (Heart and mouth and deed and life) move to joyous dance rhythms in praise of God. Many of the brilliant secular cantatas document events in the lives and the deaths of the rulers under whom Bach worked. Others, such as the "Coffee" and "Peasant" cantatas, and the magnificent *Geschwinde, ihr wirbelnden Wind,* known in English as the "Contest Between Phoebus and Pan" (with a libretto by Henrici) are something else altogether—comic masterworks, operas in all but name.

Although they are less popular than Bach's instrumental music, a case could be made that the cantatas stand as the most significant portion of his oeuvre. The musicologist Christoph Wolff observes that "the *St. Matthew Passion,* which formed the pinnacle of the vocal works composed by Bach for the Leipzig churches, reached its lofty heights on shoulders of his earlier works."[5] The *Passions* are built like cantatas on a much bigger scale, and in some of the cantatas we can hear the *Passions* encapsulated. Getting to know the cantatas, daunting though that task may seem, will enhance any listener's understanding of the Passions, and constitutes a worthwhile end in and of itself. Surely that peculiarly dedicated subgroup of Bach lovers who listen lovingly to the cantatas are best equipped to deal with the mega-cantata, oratorio form of the Passions.

Bach's obituary states that he composed five Passion settings. Of these, only the *St. Matthew*, first performed during the Holy Week of 1727, and the *St. John Passion* of three years earlier survive. Henrici's libretto for the *St. Mark Passion* of 1731 has survived; Bach's music, however, remains lost. It is known that this last work drew on music Bach had already written, in particular the *Trauerode* (Funeral ode), a cantata from 1727. The recycling of old material was a common practice among composers of the era, Handel being the best-known adapter of earlier work. The *St. Luke Passion* is a work by an unknown composer that Bach copied out for performance around 1730 and to which he made a few additions. There was also another Passion, now lost, that Bach wrote in Weimar in 1717. Bach is known to have led performances of Passion settings by other composers several times over the course of his twenty-seven-year tenure as cantor of St. Thomas's Church in Leipzig. The fifth Passion mentioned in the obituary is most likely the lost Weimar

---

5. Christoph Wolff, *Johann Sebastian Bach*, p. 288.

Passion, or possibly one by another composer, which the writer assumed was Bach's.

It is fair to assume that, had the *St. Matthew Passion* been lost, the *St. John* would be regarded as one of Bach's greatest works, rather than standing in the shadow of its companion. The *St. Matthew* is indisputably the greater work, but the *St. John* is a magnificent conception, marred though it may be by its weaker libretto. Bach learned a great deal from writing the *St. John* that he would put to use several years later as he set to work on its successor, this time armed with Henrici's excellent, unified text.

The *St. John Passion* is set, like most Passions of the day, to a combination of Biblical text, hymnlike chorales that were familiar to Lutheran listeners, and Pietistic texts by contemporary poets which Bach set as arias, choruses, or, in one instance, an aria with choral interjections. It is unclear whether Bach assembled the text of the *St. John Passion* himself, with a writer's help, or whether it was prepared for him by a poet, but it seems more patched together and less artfully paced than the one Henrici would write for him. The spaciousness of Henrici's libretto, as well as the consistency of its patterns of action and reflection, and of soloist and chorus, displays a distinct improvement over the *St. John* text.

The Gospel according to John was the last of the four canonic Gospels to be written. Presenting Jesus as a full-fledged divinity descended to Earth, rather than merely as a "son of God" who is a passionate truth-teller, St. John thus carries a heavier theological burden than the other Gospels. It might therefore seem less suited to drama than the more straightforward narrative of *St. Matthew*. For Bach, however, the *St. John* inspired the more overtly dramatic work, the

St. Matthew being the more contemplative one. The earlier work's playing time, about fifty minutes shorter than that of the *St. Matthew Passion*, surely adds to the impression it gives of urgent forward motion and intensifies its dramatic punch.

Churning strings and moaning winds begin the vast opening chorus of *St. John Passion*—which runs about a minute longer than its *St. Matthew* counterpart—viscerally evoking an intolerable anxiety, soon confirmed by the urgent cries of the chorus ("Herr, herr, unser herrscher,"—Lord, Lord, our master) that demand the attention of the Godhead with fierce desperation. Here Bach uses a frankly theatrical strategy that contrasts powerfully with the gravity of the chorus that begins the *St. Matthew Passion*. Yet although the expressive means of the two movements may differ, they stand on equal footing on their lofty musical and spiritual planes.

"Wir setzen uns mit Tränen" (We sit in tears), the chorus that concludes the *St. Matthew*, finds its opposite in "Ruht wohl, ihr heiligen Gebeine" (Rest well, sacred limbs), the penultimate number of the *St. John*, the last being a chorale. These beautiful, deeply expressive choruses, set in the stately processional rhythm of the sarabande, are clearly cut from the same mold; again, it would seem foolish to call one superior to the other.

Any listener familiar with both Passions will have almost as many favorite moments in the *St. John Passion* as in the *St. Matthew*. "Ich folge dir gleichfalls" (I follow you with eager steps), for soprano and a pair of flutes that seem to dance their accompaniment, is irresistible; the tenor's "Ach, mein Sinn" (O, my troubled mind) is utterly operatic in the way the composer uses the convention of sharply dotted rhythms to portray with music the agitated affect of the words. Even more inspired is "Eilt, ihr angefochtnen Seeles (Hurry, you tormented souls), the dialogue for bass and chorus with a spectral accompaniment in which the rushing strings depict tormented human souls hurrying to the cross in search of peace. Bach employs instrumental tone painting to fearsome effect as well in the recitative and arioso "Und siehe da" (And look there), in which the strings shudder and rush eerily as the tenor describes the rending of the curtain of the Temple, the earthquake, and the opening of graves after Jesus's death.

Perhaps most astonishing of all is "Es ist vollbracht" (It is fulfilled), the alto's meditation on the Savior's last words. Accompanied by a single, somber-toned viola da gamba, in the dark key of B minor, and marked *molto adagio*—very slowly—the singer reflects in awestruck tones on the "end of the night of sorrow" he or she (depending on the whether the singer is a male alto or a woman) now sees for human souls. The music pauses, changing without preparation to a quick tempo and a brilliant D major as the singer praises "the hero from Judah" in a tone of triumph that is positively Handelian. The moment of visionary joy ends as suddenly as it began, and the aria ends on two rapt utterances of the opening phrase, *Es ist vollbracht.*

The shocking contrasts Bach builds into this extraordinary aria demonstrate his more theatrical rendering of the Passion as told by the writer known as St. John the Evangelist; there is nothing quite like it in the *St. Matthew Passion.* "Es ist vollbracht" is followed by another daring invention, "Mein teurer Heiland" (My dear Savior) for bass, accompanied by the chorus intoning the chorale "Jesu, der du warest tot" (Jesus, you were dead).

Every aria in the *St. John Passion* might just as easily be subjected to admiring attention. Surely as fine is Bach's rendering of the trial of Jesus, where the composer makes Pilate's unease palpable, nearly turning the superstitious Roman governor into a sympathetic figure. This long sequence, consisting of dialogue in recitative, choral interjections, and three arias, stands at the heart of the work, clearly showing the dramatic basis of Bach's conception. Some might find the *turbae*—the vigorous choral movements representing the various mobs of Jews, priests, and soldiers—a bit long and showy; those in the *St. Matthew Passion* are pithier. But few could criticize Bach's breathtaking compositional skill in "Lasset uns denn nicht zerteilen" (We must not tear this) the fleet, yet spooky chorus of the soldiers as they discuss what to do with the seamless tunic of the crucified Jesus.

Bach started to revise the *St. John Passion* immediately following its first performance in 1724, and worked on it for the rest of his life. The second performance, on Good Friday of 1725, showed significant alterations, including a new opening chorus, "O Mensch, bewein' dein' Sünde groß" (O Man, bewail your great sin), which would in 1736 take its place at the end of part I of the *St. Matthew Passion*, and a new closing chorus for the piece. The composer was clearly feeling his way toward a more satisfying, rounded structure to enhance a work of such great scope; his tinkering would pay off in the *St. Matthew*, with its frame of grand choruses that begin and conclude the work, and "O Mensch, bewein' dein' Sünde groß" standing as a pillar at its center, the end of part I.

The third version, dating probably to 1728, included minor changes. In the late 1730s, Bach embarked on a complete revision, breaking off work for unknown reasons about halfway through part I. As late as 1749, Bach worked on the fourth version, reversing all earlier alterations, while augmenting the numbers of instrumentalists.

That a work of the stature of the *St. John Passion* must take second place to its sibling speaks to the near-perfection of the *St. Matthew Passion*, into which Bach put all his skill, energy, and high purpose. As with the earlier work, the composer continued to wrestle with and revise his score for many years, but he learned from the *St. John*, tightening, intensifying, expanding, and deepening his music at every opportunity.

Christian Friedrich Henrici and Bach seem to have known each other for two or three years when the two collaborated on the *St. Matthew Passion*. The talented young poet and playwright might even have compiled the libretto of the *St. John Passion*. It is certain that Henrici wrote the libretto for a wedding cantata that Bach composed in 1725, so the acquaintance of the two may be dated safely to that year. In any case, Bach clearly respected the capabilities of his collaborator, writing Henrici's name on the title page of the score.

Little is known of the manner in which Bach and Henrici worked, but the composer's influence on the text seems unmistakable. Unlike the uneven text of the *St. John Passion*, this libretto is consistent in imagery, and is at once tighter and broader than the *St. John* pastiche. The integration of religious ideas, text, and music is absolute. The work also displays an admirable symmetry of layout, in which the six great scenes, subdivided into fifteen incidents from the biblical narrative, receive commentary in the form of twenty-eight arias to new texts by Henrici and twelve Lutheran chorales. And, even though Bach was influenced deeply by operatic affects, the learned composer endowed the *St. Matthew Passion* with a wealth of compositional styles, including contrapuntal and liturgical techniques that place the oratorio in a class of its own.

Perhaps the most outstanding example of Bach's singular creative vision of the *St. Matthew Passion* is his use of two orchestras and choruses. He did this to clarify the sound of the big opening and closing movements, in which the choruses call and respond to each other. Henrici could only have written these antiphonal sequences into his text at Bach's request. There is precedent in some sophisticated Venetian church music for antiphonal effects, but Bach's use of the technique in the Leipzig of 1727 was wildly ambitious and must have posed exceptional challenges for the musicians and listeners of the day. We hear them today as urgent and deeply moving; Bach's epic music gives their utterances the gravity of classical tragedy.

Bach's instrumental ensembles are chamber orchestras. The composer wanted a dark sound for this dark work, so there are no brass instruments, and certainly no percussion to shatter the delicate sonic web. Bach specifies for each of his two orchestras two recorders and two transverse flutes; rounding out the winds are an elaborate group of oboes. Both orchestras have one standard oboe each, and the first ensemble also has one *oboe d'amore*, a cousin of the standard instrument pitched a minor third lower, and two *oboi da caccia*, a predecessor of the English horn, now mostly obsolete aside from its use here. The sound of these oboes, subtly varied and reminiscent of the human voice in their plangent tone colors, is a crucial element in the work. The string ensembles consist of two groups of violins and a viola section, whose size varies according to the discretion of the conductor; each orchestra has a viola da gamba, a gentle-toned predecessor of the cello, and a continuo group under-pins each orchestra. These Baroque bass sections, which guide the rhythm and harmony, consist of a cello, a double bass, and an organ or harpsichord, to which some conduc-tors add a bassoon.

The fast-moving choruses for the crowd are known as *turbae*, the Latin word for "crowd" that is the root of the words "turbulent" and "disturb," which evokes the unruly mobs, usually portrayed as Jews, clamoring for Jesus's death, and whose violent outbursts provide some of the most exciting and memorable moments for first time listeners. The undeniable anti-Semitism in these passages now seems an unfortunate, but deeply rooted aspect of this great work, of which they represent an essential part.

The twelve "plain" chorale hymns (thirteen if one counts the one embedded into the tenor's recitative "O Schmerz!" in part I) interspersed throughout the *St. Matthew Passion* serve several functions: since every listener in St. Thomas Church knew every chorale by heart, they were surely islands of familiarity amid what was as bold a score as any-one in the Leipzig of 1727 had heard. A deeper aspect of the familiarity of the chorales was that on every repetition, they evoked the community of the worshippers. Their closed form and musical stability also serve to balance the aggres-sive, sometimes shocking turbae.[6] Further to unify the piece,

---

6. Alberto Basso, notes to Harmonia Mundi CD 951676, p. 18.

Bach deployed one chorale melody five times, another three times, and a third one twice. Bach transcribed hundreds of Lutheran chorales, sometimes drawing criticism for adding confusing, highly expressive and "foreign" harmonies when he played his transcriptions on the organ.[7] Those chorales Bach selected for the *St. Matthew Passion* are not merely transcribed, but fundamentally recomposed for their new role in this grand musical drama, remaking them all into highly—sometimes shockingly—expressive music. Formally and aesthetically they are highly evolved from their rough origins as Sunday church hymns.

Bach's approach to recitative (the passages in prose, generally either narrative or dialogue) in the *St. Matthew Passion* seems infinitely flexible and resourceful. Perhaps most immediately memorable are the calm string accompaniments to all the recitatives sung by Jesus, except for the final one on the cross. Even in the refined musical and spiritual universe of the *St. Matthew Passion*, the Savior's words stand out, stirring the listener's empathy with their nobility of tone. Passion settings by earlier composers, most notably Johann Sebastiani,[8] have been cited as Bach's forerunners in this practice; but these works are lost or rarely performed.

For the other characters, Bach developed a wide range of other recitative styles to suit his dramatic strategy. The Evangelist sings his text in what is known as the *stylus luxurians*[9] (luxuriant style), a form used by Passion composers of the era that is slower and more clearly inflected and emphatic than the quick, light, almost spoken *secco* (dry) recitative

---

7. Wolff, *Johann Sebastian Bach*, p. 85.
8. Mann, p. 2.
9. Martin Geck, *Johann Sebastian Bach: Life and Work*, p. 408.

of operatic prose. Finally, there are eleven more elaborate passages Bach devised to link passionately declaimed introductory texts with the meditative arias (and one duet) that follow. They are free in form but closely related to the musical material of the arias, and Bach weaves their dense, uniform textures from instrumental combinations that are unusual and expressive. These passages are referred to by the term *motivic accompagnato*.[10] Much scholarship has been devoted to these remarkable sections alone, which are without doubt more than recitatives, as Bach modestly categorized them, but not full-fledged arias.

Fifteen arias, spread fairly evenly over the *St. Matthew Passion*, form what many admirers consider the soul of the work; they also occupy nearly half the running time of the piece, forming its largest musical element. None of these is a setting of a biblical text: Bach wrote all the arias to poems by Henrici. Often confusingly described as "madrigalesque," their verse form, passionate and subjective language, as well as their nonliturgical sources, more closely resemble those of the secular madrigal than religious texts. In this sense, they reflect the Pietistic bent of the librettist and composer, and the affect-driven aesthetic of Baroque art. Both Pietism and affect are abundantly displayed, for example, in the very first aria, "Buss und reu" (Penance and remorse) sung by the alto accompanied by a pair of flutes. In this gravely beautiful piece, the inward intensity of Bach's music closely follows Henrici's condensed, image-heavy text of just eighteen words.

Bach conceived "Buss und reu" in the popular, straightforward form called *da capo*, meaning "from the beginning," in Italian. Da capo arias begin with a memorable melody

---

10. Ibid., p. 409.

before moving to a middle section; the first part is then repeated from the beginning. Another way of describing these arias would be ABA, where the opening and closing sections are essentially identical. Singers in the seventeenth and eighteenth centuries typically embroidered the repetitions of opening sections with grace notes and runs to show off their taste and vocal capabilities. This custom disturbs modern listeners and is rarely employed now, but the operatically oriented Handel expected it, and while it is possible that tasteful vocal embellishments pleased Bach, he preferred to compose his own ornamentation and fix it in his scores rather than leave it to the performer.[11] Da capo arias were vastly popular with composers, singers, and audiences of the day. The form has had a long, productive life, remaining useful to writers of popular songs.

Five of the arias in the *St. Matthew Passion* are in da capo form. Like "Buss und reu," the other four are also intimate lyrical reflections, with chamber-sized instrumental accompaniments. Three arias on a larger scale receive the most elaborate and dramatic settings, with the singers getting more support from the orchestras, choruses, and smaller instrumental groups, but each of these three is different in shape and sound.

Bach wrote the remaining seven in what is known as a "through-composed" style, which means that he wrote out every note to be played, as these arias do not have repeated sections as in da capo arias. But the unity within this fascinating category ends there: two arias are very quiet, intimate pieces in which the singer is accompanied

---

11. Charles Rosen, "Keyboard Music of Bach and Handel," pp. 30–31.

by a solo instrument and continuo, while others resemble in their individual shapes the da capo pieces. Bach gave "Erbarme dich" (Have mercy), the long, sublime aria in part II for alto, accompanied by solo violin over a plucked cello, its own sound and feeling. The composer drew from a wide and infinitely subtle palette of sounds, textures, and emotions, ensuring not only that his music enhances the meaning of Henrici's texts, but also that no two arias sound alike.

The *St. Matthew Passion* perhaps strikes a listener getting acquainted with the work with its massive strength and the profundity of its religious feeling. But the effort to which Bach went in varying the musical texture and pacing soon becomes evident, allowing listeners to appreciate the score for the composer's delicacy and attention to detail. Unlike Handel, a master of broad effects, Bach built his compositions from an large number of details; yet he also knew how to pitch these toward the big moment, of which the *St. Matthew Passion* has a fair share. Many who know the work well share an overall impression of its boldness and freedom of expression, elements that derive, paradoxically, from Bach's artistic discipline, technical mastery, and painstaking management of his material.

Comparing Bach's two surviving Passions, the German musicologist Martin Geck writes that in the later, greater work "Bach takes a giant step toward classicism."[12] Geck does not mean that in the *St. Matthew Passion* Bach somehow anticipates Haydn, Mozart, or Beethoven stylistically, or foreshadows the Viennese titans except indirectly, or sounds

---

12. Geck, p. 402.

in any way like anyone other than himself at his very best and his most characteristic. Rather, Geck is suggesting that in the St. Matthew Passion Bach achieves a structural spaciousness and equilibrium of expression that are "classical" in their restraint, symmetry, and purity. The elegiac poise of the St. Matthew Passion, into which sorrow and meditation are seamlessly woven, seems worlds apart from the surging and tortured affects of the St. John Passion, wonderful though that more dramatically conceived work of only a couple of years earlier surely is.

After its premiere on April 11, 1727, the St. Matthew Passion appears to have been performed on no more than three Good Fridays during the composer's lifetime: in 1729 (once thought to be the first performance until musicologist Joshua Rifkin persuasively argued for the earlier date) and possibly in 1736 and 1744. No two versions were identical, and Bach's revisions, while less extensive than those he performed on the St. John Passion, were just as radical in their way.

After presumably thinking and tinkering over the years, Bach made major changes to the score of the St. Matthew Passion in 1736. He replaced a chorale at the end of part I with the big chorus "O Mensch, bewein' dein' Sünde groß" from the St. John Passion, fortified the two orchestras a bit, and gave each half its own organ-backed continuo section, where before one had served for all the performers. He also made minor rhythmic adjustments to the opening chorus, and wove in, above the rest in a new conception of matchless power and boldness, the traditional Lutheran chorale melody "O Lamm Gottes unschuldig," for boy sopranos singing in a separate overhead choir loft. Any changes Bach made were to augment the monumentality of a work already immense in its scale, depth, and scope.

To Bach himself, the *St. Matthew Passion* clearly represented a high water mark. It was referred to in his household as *"der grosse Passion"*—the great Passion. In 1736, the year he made his only significant revisions, Bach also undertook the formidable task of penning a score he saw as complete and final. The incorporation of the alterations of that year renders these definitive; that a man as busy as Bach made the time to sit for the many, many hours the transcribing surely demanded speaks to his own regard for the work, which he foresaw would be valuable for generations of listeners to come. Bach wanted, therefore, to create an "archival copy" of the *St. Matthew Passion*,[13] as he would with the other compositions he considered seminal, including the sonatas and partitas for solo violin and the *Well-Tempered Clavier*.

Bach seems to have used the most expensive paper he could buy,[14] as well as two inks, red for all biblical text and that of the new chorale "O Lamm Gottes unschuldig" added to the opening, and a dark brown for the rest. Some later damage to the score he carefully repaired.[15] According to Wolff,

> There is no comparable manuscript score from Bach's hand that is so carefully laid out and written in two colors of ink. . . . It could not be more evident that in 1736 Bach considered this score as his most significant

---

13. Wolff, *Johann Sebastian Bach*, p. 457.
14. Geck, p. 32.
15. Wolff, citing Alfred Dürr, *Johann Sebstian Bach*, p. 298.

work. . . . [W]hile Bach could hardly imagine that the "great Passion," more than any of his other works, would make history in the truest sense of the word, he knew full well from the earliest planning stages that this composition would be special—indeed, that nothing like it had ever been attempted before.[16]

Bach's love and respect for his masterpiece must be moving to lovers of his music, most of whom would surrender at least an unimportant organ or limb for a look at his own definitive, painstakingly transcribed score of the *St. Matthew Passion*. This treasure now sits deteriorating in the Staatsbibliothek—the State Library—in Berlin, where careful efforts are underway to rescue it.

Bach was famous among musicians and lovers of music in the music-loving central Germany of his day, but not all of his activities were chronicled, like those of the princes he worked for—most of whom are now known more for the high honor of having been his patron than for accomplishments of their own. The image of a supreme artist like Bach writing a cantata for next Sunday's church service and pleading for money to repair a harpsichord, one eye fixed all the while on eternity, puts the notion of artistic immortality into a perspective that is troubling yet familiar. That Bach could live and work in relative obscurity is hard to believe; that important works by the composer considered by many the greatest of all are lost is breathtakingly painful to consider. But so it is: there are large gaps in Bach's biography.

---

16. Wolff, *Johann Sebastian Bach*, p. 298.

Biography, however, is not the purpose of this study, and there are already fine biographies that thoroughly cover the peculiar mix of minutiae and educated guesswork that comprises what is known about Bach's life. The basics are these: The Bach family, whose first recorded member was Veit Bach, (born probably in Moravia or Slovakia some time in the early sixteenth century), had been musical for a century before the birth of Johann Sebastian. The family name, which may have been a corruption of the word for baker (*backer*) means "brook" in German, provoking Beethoven's lovely, reverent pun "not 'Brook,' but 'Ocean,' should be his [Johann Sebastian's] name."

Johann Sebastian Bach was born in the small Thuringian village of Eisenach on March 21, 1685 to Johann Ambrosius Bach, the multitalented town musician, and Maria Elisabeth Bach. Johann Sebastian's mother and father died in 1694 and 1695, respectively. The young Bach and his brother Johann Jacob went to live with their oldest brother Johann Christoph, an organist in the small city of Ohrdruf.

In 1700 Bach, then fifteen, was sent to school in the north German city of Lüneburg, near Hamburg, where he was able to hear some of the great organists of the region. In 1703 he was employed as a musician at the little ducal court of Saxe-Weimar; later that year he was hired as organist at the New Church of Arnstadt, another small town in Thuringia. Two years later, Bach took an extended leave in the Baltic port of Lübeck, where he visited Dietrich Buxtehude, the greatest German organist before Bach himself. In the first of many such instances in his life, Bach clashed with his employers, putting his musical education ahead of his work by overstaying his allowed leave in Lübeck. By this time,

Bach was already famous as a virtuoso on the organ, the chief source of his fame during his lifetime. He was also respected as an authority on the construction of the complex instrument, an expertise for he would be well paid many times over the course of his career. Bach extended his virtuosity to all keyboard instruments, playing the violin and viola well too.

In 1707 the young composer was hired as an organist at St. Blasius's Church in Mühlhausen, yet another small city in Thuringia. While working there he married his first wife, Maria Barbara Bach, a cousin, with whom he would have seven children over the course of thirteen years before her early and unexpected death in 1720 while Bach was away with his employer, the Prince of Anhalt-Cöthen. It was in Mühlhausen that Bach composed his first cantatas. In the following year, Bach and his wife moved to Weimar, where Bach was the newly appointed organist to the Duke of Weimar. There is some evidence that Bach may have composed many of his grand and fiery masterworks for organ there. In Weimar, too, most of his children with Maria Barbara were born, including Wilhelm Friedemann and Carl Philipp Emmanuel, fine composers on their own. Bach, though, clashed with a successor of the duke who had hired him, landing the stubborn, hot-tempered composer in jail for a full month in November and December of 1717.

The next stop for Bach and his family was the little Saxon principality of Anhalt-Cöthen, where the composer flourished and was well paid under the patronage of a youthful, music-loving prince. This sojourn proved phenomenally productive, for it was during the six years Bach spent there from 1717 to 1723 that he found maturity as a composer. In Cöthen, composing ecclesiastic and occasional cantatas were not Bach's only activities; he studied music of Italian masters, broadening his own style considerably, and wrote many of his best known instrumental works. These include the peerless sonatas and partitas for solo violin, suites for solo cello, the sonatas for violin and continuo, the *Brandenburg Concerti*, the Two- and Three-Part Inventions for keyboard, and book 1 of the *Well-Tempered Clavier*.

Eighteen months after the death of Bach's wife Maria Barbara in 1720 he married the singer Anna Magdalena Wilcke, sixteen years his junior and a gifted musician in her own right, who would be his mate and companion for the rest of his life. This marvelous, spirited, patient woman (she became pregnant thirteen times) is secondary to her husband in his biographies, but she comes across as warmhearted, energetic, and immensely likable, fully up to the demanding job of wife to a great man. It was for Anna Magdalena that Bach wrote two notebooks of little keyboard studies—the *Anna Magdalena Notebooks* that carry her name. For her part, Anna Magdalena was the transcriber of the copies of many of the master's greatest works that have survived, including the solo music for violin and cello, much of the *Well-Tempered Clavier*, and portions of the B-minor Mass. She and Bach loved each other dearly, and she was privileged to be one of the earliest connoisseurs of his music.

Bach lobbied for the position of *kantor* (choir director) of the St. Thomas Church in Leipzig, and in early 1723 he moved there with his family. Though the title sounds insignificant, the job was in fact one of the most prestigious in German music at the time,[17] comparable in stature,

---

17. Christoff Wolff, *The New Grove Bach Family*, p. 81.

perhaps, to being music director of one of the major American symphony orchestras, albeit without the international fame. Bach's new responsibilities were onerous, encompassing the production of cycles of weekly cantatas for the church year, plus occasional cantatas—often on short notice—to mark secular events, as well as a far greater load of teaching, training, and managerial duties. It was a difficult assignment, even for a man of Bach's immense energies and far-ranging skills. The composer, who was consistently combative when called upon to compromise the integrity of the music he wrote and performed, would clash frequently and bitterly with the town council and other Leipzig functionaries.

These were the years during which Bach began to produce his largest-scale masterworks, the *Magnificat* of 1723; the *St. John Passion* of 1723–1724, first performed in the latter year; and the *St. Matthew Passion* of three years later. The year 1731 saw the publication of the first volume of the *Clavier-Übung*, a collection of works for keyboard that included the partitas; other volumes, one including the magnificent *French Overture*—a seventh keyboard partita— and the *Italian Concerto* came out in 1735. The fourth volume, which includes the *Goldberg Variations*, would follow in 1741. The *Christmas Oratorio*, a spectacular assemblage of six reworked cantatas, was introduced in the holiday season of 1734–1735. Bach's cantata production, prolific in the early Leipzig years, appears to have become more occasional and somewhat less systematic, though every bit as glorious; in 1733, Bach wrote the first portions of what would eventually become the Mass in B minor in honor of the Catholic Elector of Saxony.

Bach's life during his twenty-seven years in Leipzig involved a surprising amount of travel on personal business, including paid consultancies on the construction and rebuilding of organs in many central German cities. Bach kept connections to Cöthen, where he returned to lead performances several times in the 1720s. There were also many visits to Dresden, the capital of Saxony. There he viewed many operas—forbidden in the more puritanical atmosphere of Lutheran Leipzig—which he clearly adored. He also successfully cultivated the patronage of the Saxon royal family, which in 1737 named him court composer.

These outside jobs and the Saxon appointment seem to have freed Bach at least partially from the misery of his amply documented conflicts with Leipzig authorities. By 1730, however, Bach was so discouraged that he was complaining in writing that he might need to find another position.[18] He clashed with his Leipzig bosses over everything from the cost of repairing a harpsichord to the qualifications of the musicians and singers he directed; an appalling personal feud erupted in 1736 with a one-time friend, Johann August Ernesti, rector of St. Thomas, into which the town council needed to intervene.

Even the most casual listener can sense in Bach's music an intellectual coherence of a rare focus and intensity, the product of a singular mind. Bach knew it, too; and as his sense of self-worth and place in musical history combined with his greater financial independence during his Leipzig years, he conceived and created encyclopedic works, or groups of works, like some of those he had written in Cöthen, that

---

18. Wolff, *Johann Sebastian Bach*, p. 350.

defined once and for all the expressive and formal limits of a musical idea. These included explorations of the expressive possibilities of two- and three-voice keyboard writing (in every key practically available at the time) in the *Inventions* and *Sinfonias*, or the extroverted French and Italianate grandeur of the partitas, or his definitive explorations of pure counterpoint in *A Musical Offering* and *The Art of Fugue*. These also included the ultimate oratorio Passion, the *St. Matthew Passion*, after which most composers found it prudent to give the form a wide berth for two hundred years.

In the last twenty-five years of his life, Bach seemed to find ways to remove himself from the day-to-day aggravations of his Leipzig responsibilities and to focus on these big ideas, though he was constitutionally incapable of genuine aloofness: as late as 1749 he lashed out furiously at a local critic who mocked his learned style as old-fashioned. The combination of Bach's fame, his access to the Elector of Saxony, and his relative financial independence apparently placed him beyond the reach of the Leipzig authorities, no matter how difficult many of them found him. Thus he dutifully fulfilled his Leipzig duties, but never at the expense of his continuing professional education, enjoyment, and especially the creation of his mighty musical compendia. The man had much to say, and he worked hard to say it.

In 1747 Bach visited Frederick II "the Great," King of Prussia, in Berlin. The aging master showed no loss of acuity as he improvised a fugue on a theme by the king, followed by a six-part fugue on a theme of his own, to the astonishment of all present. Bach later developed this theme into *A Musical Offering*, a brilliant display of contrapuntal writing, as well as a trio sonata in a more modern style. Counterpoint was a central concern of Bach's in his last years as he worked on *The Art of Fugue*, one of the great abstract musical works, which he did not finish. He also completed his B-minor Mass in 1749. For most of his life Bach was extremely robust, but in the late 1740s his health seems to have failed fairly quickly. He nearly died in the summer of 1749, and had already lost his eyesight, perhaps from diabetes. He was operated on twice in early 1750 by the same well-known surgeon who had attempted to restore Handel's eyesight; a brief improvement in Bach's vision was followed, in July, by a stroke; Bach died on the evening of July 28, 1750.

Disputes with employers and others form an important part of the record of Bach's professional life that has come down to us, giving an impression of his character that may be somewhat exaggerated. That Bach had a fiery temperament is indisputable—as a man of driving ambition and the highest intellect he did not suffer fools gladly; how could he? But evidence suggests other sides to the man, including his lusty creative energy, which can be heard in the driving motion of his music, and extrapolated from the twenty children he fathered and the unremitting hard work with which he produced hundreds of works of an extraordinarily high and even quality. His fondness for his pipe, hard cider, wine (which he described in a letter as "a noble gift of God"[19]), brandy, and beer is well documented, and his humor, at once lordly and earthy, shows itself clearly in the wonderful secular cantatas and the obscene lyrics he

---

19. Ibid., p. 395.

liked to drop into well-known melodies at well-lubricated family gatherings.

Yet this great man was above arrogance, as his son Carl Philip Emanuel wrote in 1788, recalling a keyboard-playing contest of years earlier in which Bach crushed Louis Marchand, his French rival. His father did not like to talk about the incident, C. P. E. Bach noted, adding that J. H. Bach was never "a challenging musical braggart," and was "anything but proud of his qualities and never let anyone feel his own superiority."[20]

It is heartening to consider the affection and respect with which Bach's sons remembered him years later. As C. P. E. Bach told the early biographer Johann Nikolaus Forkel in explanation of the lack of letters and other written records of his father's life,

> With his many activities he hardly had time for the most necessary correspondence, and accordingly would not indulge in lengthy written exchanges. But he had the more opportunity to talk personally to good people, since his house was like a pigeonry [a pigeon-coop], and just as full of life. Association with him was pleasant for every-one, and often very edifying.[21]

The musical legacy of the Bach family continued for a generation after the death of its most famous member. None of Bach's composing sons wrote in counterpoint like their father but worked, reasonably enough, in the classical style dominant during their own lives. Wilhelm Friedemann, the eldest son, began his career promisingly in Dresden

---

20. Ibid., p. 180.
21. Ibid., p. 408.

as one of the finest church organists of his day, but seems to have drifted into chronic unemployment as he reached middle age, dying impoverished in Berlin. Johann Christian Bach worked first in Milan, then in London, because of which fact he was known as "the English Bach" or "the London Bach." Johann Christian composed opera in the mainstream Italian style, which were, however, admired by Haydn, Mozart, and Beethoven for their charming melodies and polished orchestration.

The work of Carl Phillip Emanuel holds up best of all. He deserves credit as one of the masters of classical sonata form, and composed many works for keyboard that are still played, especially by students; he was a master of what was known as the "sensitive style," marked by abrupt changes of mood and a highly pitched emotionalism. Complex, passionate, and of a high technical finish, Emmanuel's music has much in common with that of his mighty father, but in the classical, rather than the contrapuntal, style. He also wrote a landmark treatise on keyboard style, the *Essay on the True Art of Playing Keyboard Instruments*, which is still useful, respected, and read with pleasure, too.

Chapter 2

 _art I_

THE FIRST AND SHORTER of the two immense pan-
els that form the diptych of the *St. Matthew Passion* covers
the events narrated in verses 3 through 56 of chapter 26 of
the Gospel. The action opens with Jesus telling his disciples
how he wants to prepare for the feast of the Passover, and
then continues through his anointment in Bethany, the Last
Supper, his prayers in the Garden of Gethsemane, and his
abandonment by Peter and the other followers. The final
incident portrayed is his betrayal by Judas Iscariot and arrest
by Roman soldiers.

Bach divides these events into five scenes of considerable dramatic impact, with eighteen recitatives and *turbae*
choruses carrying the narrative flow. Five chorales and six
arias punctuate the action, reflecting on the Savior's self-
sacrifice with ever-deepening intensity; two big choruses act
as centers of gravity opening and closing the structure of
Bach's "first act."

Like most vocal compositions of more than one movement, the *St. Matthew Passion* is divided into individual
"numbers," with every chorus, recitative, chorale, and aria
receiving its own numerical designation. Thus, the opening chorus is (obviously) number 1, and a recitative for the
Evangelist and the *turbae* chorus with which it is connected
are listed in the score as 4a and 4b. This numbering of connected pieces may cause some confusion, since there are
sixty-eight movements, including those joined together,
but seventy-eight if one counts every individual movement
separately. The first part has twenty-nine numbered movements, but thirty-five individual numbers.

There is no question regarding the *St. Matthew Passion*
more uncertain and contentious than that of the number
of singers Bach had in mind for the work. The composer's
intentions are unclear; the score calls for the four standard
vocal categories (soprano, alto, tenor, and bass) for the two
choruses, from which soloists are to be drawn. The size of
the choruses on the few occasions when Bach led the work
in his lifetime is not known. A growing number of scholars
and musicians are accepting the assertion of the conductor
and scholar Joshua Rifkin, who controversially suggested in
1981 that Bach wanted and used only nine singers: one per
"group," with one more singer, a boy soprano for the opening
chorus. This question will be examined further in chapter 4,
but it is possible that its answer will never be known. Performance practice is only certain since the 1829 revival under
Felix Mendelssohn; through the nineteenth and early twentieth centuries, when conductors favored large choirs and
many soloists. In an attempt to get closer to Bach's sound,

conductors since the mid-twentieth century have continually reduced the number of choristers and solo singers to four or fewer per choir, making them double up on dramatic roles and meditative arias.

The two main characters, and the ones who do the most singing, are the Evangelist (who covers the biblical text, thus acting as narrator), sung by a tenor, and Jesus, sung by a bass or bass-baritone. Others who appear in part I include the disciples Peter and Judas (both baritones); the other disciples sung by a *turba* chorus. More characters appear in the trial of Jesus in part II.

The solos in the contemplative arias, all to texts by Henrici, are not sung by named characters, but represent the sinning but faithful Christian man and woman (Lutheran with strong Pietist leanings, of course) as they reflect and express their emotions on the events and meaning of the Passion. The opening chorus adds to the dramatis personae the metaphorical Daughters of Zion, representing the holy city of Jerusalem where Jesus died, in a grand dialogue with the Faithful.[22] One must always bear in mind that the scientific revolution was barely underway when the *St. Matthew Passion* was first performed, and that Bach and his original listeners viewed the world in religious, rather than empirical or skeptical, terms. Thus Bach's Leipzig audience would have understood the meanings of the allegorical figures and the dialogue of the opening chorus, "Kommt, ihr Töchter" (Come, you Daughters), and would not have been puzzled, as we may feel today at their obscurity and apparent strangeness. Henrici's libretto opens with the Faithful

---

22. Ibid., p. 302.

calling the Daughters of Zion: "Come, you Daughters, help us lament," they sing. "Behold." "Whom?" the Daughters ask. "The Bridegroom," the Faithful answer, employing another metaphor for Jesus. "See him!" call the Faithful; "How?" the Daughters of Zion ask. "Like a Lamb," the Faithful reply. "See!" the Faithful call; "What?" The Daughters ask. "His patience." Again the Faithful call out: "Look!" "Where?" "There, at our guilt," they continue. The groups join together at last to sing the final two lines: "See him, out of love and graciousness, carrying the wood of the cross."

Above this grandiose call-and-response sequence soars a high-soprano chorus, singing the chorale meolody "O Lamm Gottes unschuldig": "O innocent Lamb of God," they sing, "slaughtered on the stem of the cross, always found patient, though despised. All sin have you borne, else we must have despaired. Have mercy on us, o Jesus!" This is the message of the highly relevant and inspired overlay (called the "Lutheran *Agnus Dei*") that Bach applied to "Kommt, ihr Töchter" in 1736. Although an independent musical idea, "O Lamm Gottes unschuldig" is absolutely integral to the movement.

These lyrics follow the text of the better-known Latin version from the Mass fairly closely, although the Catholic version is shorter and more plangent: "Lamb of God, who takes away the sins of the world, have mercy on us!" Bach would set it profoundly in the B-minor Mass. Bach's magnificent cantata *Wachet auf, ruft uns die Stimme* is based on the nearly identical theme of Jerusalem preparing for the coming of its bridegroom, the man-god. There, the music bursts with excitement, while here it is heavy with pain.

Bach's purpose in writing "Kommt, ihr Töchter" is the expression of spiritual guilt—not an easy theme to enunciate.

This spiritual guilt is quite different, for example, from Alfredo's remorse for his misbehavior in act 2 of *La Traviata*, perfectly articulated by Verdi; it is, instead, the burning awareness of the community of the faithful meditating on their narrow escape from damnation, and their horror at the suffering endured by the Savior for the sake of an unworthy humanity. These themes may seem too abstract to be inspiring, but Bach forged Lutheran theology into music anyone might understand. One does not have to be a believer to hear in Bach's music the mystery of suffering, and the tragic riddle of existence itself. The listener's sense of purged exaltation at the end of "Kommt, ihr Töchter" is the measure of Bach's artistic success at expressing his tragic vision. Even those who know every note find more depth on every listening, and still never touch bottom. In the oceanic sublimity of "Kommt, ihr Töchter" we all must swim for our lives.

Indeed, so vast, profound, and potent is "Kommt, ihr Töchter" that it would make a more than adequate subject for a book itself; no survey can do more than scratch its surface, as with the countless other flawless, diamond-hard facets of the *St. Matthew Passion*. Nevertheless, first-time and relatively inexperienced listeners should listen for the demarcations of its three broad sections, welded though they are into a seamless whole; they should be aware, further, that, like most of Bach's music, "Kommt, ihr Töchter" is contrapuntally conceived, with interwoven lines of equal importance.

Both orchestras and choruses play and sing, respectively, and the additional soprano chorus makes its contribution almost separately. Bach's basic key is a dark E minor; the beat is the long, loping, usually graceful 12/8 of a *pastorale* (like the last movement of Corelli's "Christmas Concerto," which Bach probably knew, or the last movement of his own Brandenburg Concerto no. 6), but which in this piece he makes pulse and throb terribly. Bach may have chosen this pastoral beat specifically for its traditional association with the piping "shepherds abiding in the field, keeping watch over their flock by night" (Luke 2:8) as he did with the Christmas chorale *Vom Himmel hoch* (From heaven above), and the lilting instrumental *Sinfonia* that opens part II of the *Christmas Oratorio*. Its metaphorical meaning suggests the innocence of humanity, of the loss of that innocence through sin, and the willing self-sacrifice of the Savior, shepherd of the nearly lost flock.

More than one commentator has heard in this chorus a figurative march of the faithful to Golgotha, the locus of sacrifice and salvation, and world navel of Christian theology. Bach liked the metaphor, which also animates the great aria for bass and chorus, "Eilt, ihr angefochtnen Seelen," in the *St. John Passion*, which urges the beleaguered to "hurry to the hill of the cross, where your powers will be revived." That chorus, light-footed and hopeful, is a far cry from the limping, agonized tread of "Kommt, ihr Töchter." Surely the idea in Bach's mind was also of portraying in music the terrible march that brought Jesus himself there. These ideas may help partially to explain Bach's surprising use of a normally lyrical time signature for this desperate procession. Such are but a few of the complexities Bach creates for us before we have heard a note.

"Kommt, ihr Töchter" begins with a dark, surging tide of full orchestral sound above the terrible, fixed pulsing of the two continuos (cellos, double-bass, and organs) on a low E with a long, winding, melody that is sorrowful, yet which also bites, stings, and punishes. Bach's four-part harmony, while strict and pure, is nevertheless thick, clotted, and richly expressive with chromatic movement and suspensions. The violins sigh; the bass stalks upward in a grand gesture, unleashing some of the material's pent-up energy. The first chorus enters in a huge, sculptural rising figure that then seems to float gravely downward for the next thirteen bars. The long measures of sweeping 12/8 beat seem to extend the phrases infinitely.

The rising figure in the bass returns; two long bars later, the dialogue with the second chorus begins, its contribution at first limited to the interjected, single-word questions described above. The texture throughout is thick, and one feels afloat in a vast ocean created by the swaying rhythm. Suddenly, the soprano chorus Bach added in 1736 enters with the even, sturdy, sonorous notes of the chorale "O Lamm Gottes unschuldig." Bach puts this chorale in G major, the *relative major* of E minor. This technical term means that the two keys share the same key signature of one sharp, and that to the ear they sound similar, though G major is perceived as bright and E minor as dark or sad. The chorale, therefore, does not clash with the tonality of the big chorus but complements it, cutting through like a beam of light. The clear, bright sound of the soprano choir (whether sung by women or boys) also amplifies the dramatic impact of this inspired addition.

The main chorus moves fully into the major key, marking the start of the middle section of the movement. The mood is hardly brighter, but the change of tonality allows the frayed nerves of Bach's listeners a bit of rest. The composer also adds further contrast, here of texture, breaking the long, tied notes that dominate the orchestral accompaniments into lighter, staccato chords. These, too, have a tidal grandeur, like smaller waves lapping across the vast groundswell of sound, breaking its surface. Above all, the plain, long notes of the soprano chorale soar like a beacon.

But the minor key returns, bringing in the reprise a feeling even heavier and more bitter than before, as the movement sweeps with unstoppable power toward its conclusion on a hard E-major chord that offers no comfort, despite its change of tonality and tone color.

As undeniably overwhelming as "Kommt, ihr Töchter" is on its own, the movement serves crucial structural purposes within the vast magnitude of the *St. Matthew Passion.* The movement functions much like the overture of a large-scale opera, such as Mozart's to *Don Giovanni,* Bellini's to *Norma,* or half a dozen of Wagner's major operatic preludes. Their large scale gives the listener an immediate sense of the dimension of the work they open, and their moods tell much about the subject matter of what will follow.

"Kommt, ihr Töchter" is also analogous to the exordium of classical epic, the poet's weighty invocation of the muse that opens works from the *Iliad* and *Odyssey* to Milton's *Paradise Lost.* Like "Kommt, ihr Töchter," the exordia of classical epics stand apart from the narratives they introduce, and, as the lofty tone of the epic exordium serves also to summon the reader, telling him or her that the poet has embarked on a work of a grand scale and a high style; so in "Kommt, ihr Töchter" Bach signals his original audience of worshippers—and listeners of ages to come—of his high purpose in the *St. Matthew Passion.*

Bach begins that narrative immediately, however, with a recitative. The Evangelist picks up the story in the middle, from Matthew 26:1–2, in which Jesus tells his disciples that in two days when Passover begins, the "Son of Man" (that is, Jesus himself) will be arrested and crucified. The Evangelist sings in a sober, pious tone, befitting the material; from Jesus's first note, a string quartet envelops his words in the soft halo of sound accorded to no other personage, setting him apart. Almost every syllable in the recitatives is sung to a single note, but here Bach sets the word "crucified" to a twisting series of notes called a melisma that expresses the cruelty of the punishment, as well as Jesus's dread of it. This device is one of many musical methods Bach uses throughout the *Passion* to heighten the meaning and power of words.

The next number is the first separate chorale, "Herzliebster Jesu" (Dearest Jesus). The chorus asks Jesus rhetorically but gravely, "Dear Lord Jesus, what have you done wrong that such a harsh fate is pronounced? What is your guilt, into what sort of misdeeds have you fallen?" Here Bach uses the traditional chorale melody and text together, but he will set the texts of two other chorales to this same melody over the course of the *St. Matthew Passion*, tying the work together and creating points of familiarity for listeners.

The chorales, interspersed regularly through the *Passion*, serve as harbors of sorrowful rest as the drama progresses. They are also the most tight and closed elements, at least formally, of this daring work, their words moving in their predictable pattern of rhetorical question and response, while the music follows, usually opening and closing in the same key and reaching the point of greatest tension at their central cadence. Their stability makes sturdy building blocks among the more experimental choruses and arias, even though Bach restlessly finds ways to destabilize the chorales as well. In "Herzliebster Jesu" such activity is fairly mild, limited to notes side-slipping chromatically, expressing grief.

The next five numbers, all brief, move the story ahead. First comes an information-packed recitative in which the Evangelist relates the plotting of the high priests against Jesus (26:3–5). When one priest cautions against having him killed on Passover, saying, "Not on the feast day, lest there be an uproar among the people," the two choruses break into the first turba movement, in a vigorous, incisive dance rhythm, almost reminiscent of the Brandenburgs or even a concerto by Vivaldi. Over in seconds, it vividly displays the anger and destructive energy of the various mobs and plotters who wish Jesus dead.

The story moves forward with another short recitative in which the Evangelist relates Jesus's anointment by a woman in the house of Simon the leper, in Bethany (26:6–8). The disciples' indignation at what they narrow-mindedly view as a waste of costly ointment that could have been sold to raise money for the poor is expressed in the second turba chorus, which seems musically to be merely a continuation of the first. Although here Bach uses only one-half of his double chorus, he paints the Savior's followers in the same appalling colors as his enemies: they may be on his side, but they are as self-righteous and combative as the priests and elders heard moments earlier.

In the long recitative that follows, the Evangelist relates Jesus's calming of his excited followers. In tranquil tones, Jesus points out that the woman has done a good deed for him, "For ye have the poor always with you, but me ye have not always. For in that she hath poured this ointment on my body, she did it for my burial" (26:10–12). Jesus's vocal line and the notes of his string accompaniment droop, as though pulled earthward, with the word "burial."

Bach precedes "Buß und Reu" (Penance and remorse), the first aria to a text by Henrici, with one of the brief movements listed in the score as a recitative, but which is so intense and elaborate that musicologists have come to call it and its fellows "motivic accompagnatos" to differentiate them from the true recitatives sung by the Evangelist. Typically performed by the instruments that play in the arias they introduce, these remarkable passages accord those arias a special status, and far more weight within the *St. Matthew Passion* than a plain recitative could. In this one, Henrici's lyrics tie together and comment on the disciples' agitated turba, the Evangelist's recitative, and Jesus's with the verbal and musical images of "Buß und Reu." They say, in summary, "Dear Redeemer, while your disciples quarrel foolishly, this pious woman would anoint you for the grave. Allow me to pour water on your head, just as tears stream from my eyes." Although only about one minute long, the passage is of a richness typical of these inventions.

The two flutes and continuo (contrabass, cello, and organ) move in graceful step to the pictorial sensitivity of Bach's music. The alto's vocal line dips down for the word "grave" and the instrumental ensemble harmonizes with the vocal line as it again descends, like dripping water, for the words "water on your head." We will hear similar tone painting in "Buß und Reu," and the tonality of the passage stands in close relation to that of "Buß und Reu," toward which it moves in the final three bars. The rhythm here is broader and slower than the dancelike feel of the aria's beat. Thus, the motivic accompagnato prepares us for the aria to which it is linked with its instrumental color and tone painting, and with the delicate differences of its complementary key and rhythm.

"Penance and remorse grind the sinful heart in two. May the drops of my tears anoint you acceptably, faithful Jesus." These are Henrici's words that inspired Bach to the wonderful display of compositional skill that is "Buß und Reu," the first of the meditative arias in the *St. Matthew Passion*. As usual, the aria is so dense, layered, and skillfully wrought that no survey can do more than highlight a few of its wonders.

The same instrumental ensemble as in the preceding motivic accompagnato opens the piece with a piercing melody in an unmistakable dance rhythm. Both phrases of the melody end with a sighing figure that forms chief musical image of the work. The alto enters with a phrase that immediately picks up this sighing interval for the word "buß" (penance), which soon after Bach sets to a sobbing figure. Thus, the feeling—the affect—of spiritual regret is established and described unforgettably with notes, and the sighing figure (known as an *appoggiatura*) is heard over and over, making the impression of guilt seem obsessive, in an instance of Bach's profound insight into human psychology.

Bach does more tone painting in his setting of the word "knirscht" (grinds), which he sets to a sharply falling four-note phrase. But perhaps the most wonderful instance of his pictorial approach comes in the middle section: in detached notes of exquisite delicacy, the two flutes paint for our ears the very image of individual falling teardrops, carrying Henrici's words to a higher level.

Since "Buß und Reu" is in the *da capo* form, the opening section is repeated to end the piece. Given the heavyhearted text, one might sensibly expect Bach's music to be heavy, too, as with the opening chorus. But the irresistible dance rhythm, light instrumentation, and sensitivity of the music offset, rather than underline, the text. Bach understands that not every number can be weighty over the course of a long, serious work like the *St. Matthew Passion*. Since he cannot alter the nature of the subject, he shrewdly varies the textures and pacing of his music.

A short but significant recitative follows. The Evangelist tells of Judas Iscariot's plan to betray Jesus. Judas asks the priests what they will pay him to "deliver him up unto you." The priests make the infamous bargain for thirty pieces of silver. "And from that time he sought opportunity to betray him" (26:14–16). This leads directly into the next aria, "Blute nur" (Bleed on), for soprano, which reflects on Judas's deed, regarded by pious Christians as the ultimate act of treachery.

Henrici's twenty-seven-word German text is as rich in Pietistic imagery as "Buß und Reu": "Bleed on, dear heart. A child you raised, that sucked at your breast, threatens to murder its guardian: it has become a serpent." Bach accords this aria weightier treatment, however, adding to the pair of flutes and continuo of the previous aria two violins and a viola; once again he employs the da capo form. Here syncopation, the placing of rhythmic emphasis on the "wrong" beat, breaking the expected pattern of the music, is Bach's chief expressive vehicle.

The rhythmic unease begins immediately, as the flutes and violins present an intense, almost morbid melody with a ticking rhythm over broken figuration for the viola; together these make the music sound as though it limps. Rising and falling melodic patterns alternate just before the beginning of the middle section, where the horrified affect is stronger yet. There, Bach breaks up the soprano's vocal line into a sequence of disturbing, off-rhythm convolutions, adding winding melismas on the words "murder" and "serpent," and trills on "worden" (become) to mimic with notes the move-ment of the reptile. As in "Buß und Reu," the grinding sound of weeping appoggiaturas on the crucial words "heart" and "child" express the dismay and grief of the anonymous pious soul the singer represents. And, like "Buß und Reu," "Blute nur" works its way relentlessly into the mind and heart of the listener with its piercing expression of religious emotions, to which its relatively modest scale provides no obstacle.

The Evangelist, in a brief recitative, continues with the story of the Passover seder known as the Last Supper, as related in 26:17. In a beautifully flowing, gentle turba chorus unlike any other, the disciples ask Jesus, "Where wilt thou that we prepare to eat the Passover?" Jesus instructs them to tell the nameless host of the meal that he and the disciples are coming. Increasingly troubled by what he knows is to come, Jesus tells the disciples, "One of you shall betray me" (26:21). Bach changes keys for the very short but powerfully expressive recitative in which the disciples "were exceeding sorrowful, and began every one of them to say unto him, Lord, is it I?" (26:22). The last four words are sung in a short but furious turba in which the disciples, shocked and defen-sive, seem to be attacking Jesus.

Then follows, in metaphoric response, the chorale "Ich bin's": "It is I. I should atone, hands and feet bound, in hell.

The scourges and chains and all you endured, that has my soul earned." Bach sets these bitter words to the strains of the chorale "O Welt, ich muss dich lassen" (O World, I must leave you). As with the first chorale, Bach's treatment is reasonably straightforward, except that he transposes it into A-flat major, a rich-sounding key rarely employed before regulated tuning in "equal temperament" came into general use nearly a century later, opening for all musicians the full range of twenty-four keys and their colorings. Of course Bach, as an avant-gardist who had already experimented in exotic key signatures in the *Well-Tempered Clavier*, pushed tonalities to their expressive extremes again in the *St. Matthew Passion*.[23]

The long and important recitative that follows recounts in condensed form Jesus's words at his final meal, as recounted in 26:20–29. In prophetic tones and with a manifestly heavy heart, Jesus warns that one of them will betray him: "Woe unto that man . . . it had been good for that man if he had not been born" (26.24). Throughout this passage, Bach seems to emphasize Jesus's role as a prophet, having him sing in angular phrases that move forcefully downward. After Judas spectrally asks "It is I, Rabbi?" the string quartet that accompanies Jesus's words plays a drooping eight-note phrase to the Savior's strange affirmation: "Thou hast said."

After the Evangelist relates Jesus's breaking of the unleavened bread and blessing of the Passover wine, the rhythm changes for the Savior's words as he creates the mystery of the Eucharist: "Take, eat; this is my body" (26:26). Bach sets

---

23. Those interested in Bach's use of keys in the *St. Matthew Passion* would do well to read Christoph Wolff's brief but clear analysis in *Johann Sebastian Bach: The Learned Musician*, p. 301.

Jesus's words to a calm, exceptionally warm accompaniment in a long measure over a stately dance rhythm like that of a minuet, only broader. Bach makes this rhythm more explicit in the flowing, beautiful lines that follow in which Jesus tells the disciples to drink the wine "for this is my blood of the new testament, which is shed for many for the remission of sins" (26:27–28). The next verse, in which Jesus forswears "the fruit of the vine until that day when I drink it new with you in my Father's kingdom" (26:28) concludes this majestic passage. Bach's setting is of warmth and grandly flowing grace, as befits one of the founding moments of Christianity.

This awe-inspiring incident calls for a reflective aria; but Bach precedes "Ich will dir mein Herze schenken" (I will give you my heart) for soprano with a motivic accompagnato of marvelous intensity: "Although my heart swims in tears because Jesus takes leave of us, his testament gives me joy," sings the soloist, "his flesh and blood, so precious, he bequeaths into my hands. As he in this world with his own, could not think evil, so he loves them to the end." Henrici's text is convoluted and image-heavy, but Bach makes it sing with the two oboi d'amore (the slightly deeper-pitched sibling of the standard oboe) that accompany the singer in the aria, over the pulsing bass provided by the continuo.

The winds play in close-harmony triplets, the throbbing rhythmic figure in which three notes are squeezed into the space of two. Does this perhaps illustrate in notes the "swimming" of Henrici's text? Certainly its fervor suggests a breathless overflow of pious emotion, as the soprano must reach up for the notes to which Bach sets the words "although," "Jesus," "blood," and "love." On first hearing and perhaps a few thereafter, Bach's music seems almost anxious, but eventually the listener comes to hear the bursting spiritual joy expressed by the crowded press of notes.

And joy is the unmistakable affect of the aria, which opens with a bubbling, rising figure for the twining oboes in the rhythm of a pastorale. The key is a bright G major, as the soprano expresses her faith in and gratitude to Jesus, sounding like a lover in Henrici's almost erotic imagery: "I will give my heart to you, sink yourself in it, my Salvation. I will submerge myself in you. And if the world is too small for you, ah, then for me alone will you be more than world and heaven." The tone of the music throughout is cheerful, hopeful and strong.

As he often does, Bach throws the word "heart" into high relief at the singer's opening line, also highlighting "schenken" (give) with a long, joyous run of notes, and emphasizing "sink" in powerful paired phrases, one sung high, the other low. Throughout the opening sequence, Bach spins out long, overlapping melodic phrases. The middle section of this third da capo aria for soloist accompanied by paired woodwinds is more complex and angular. The oboes seem to bleat like lambs in this musical allegory of a member of the flock who has been found.

A long sequence of recitative alternating with chorales carries the Gospel drama through the events related in *Matthew* 26:30–38. The first recitative makes dramatic use of the poetic language of verses 30 through 32, in which Jesus talks to the disciples on the Mount of Olives, their ascent of which Bach marks with a rising notes for the continuo instruments. Likening his followers after his death to sheep, Jesus sings "the flock shall be scattered abroad" (26:31), as sharp figures for the strings underline his words. Bach smoothes the strings down as Jesus then tells the disciples, "After I am risen again, I will go before you into Galilee" (26:32).

The first chorale employing the tune of "Herzlich tut mich verlangen" (My heart is filled with longing), the chorale melody most favored by Bach in the work, follows. One can see why Bach uses it five times, as this rich melody evokes emotions at once somber, melancholy, hopeful, and infinitely regretful. Over the course of the *St. Matthew Passion*, Bach will put the melody through astonishing harmonic changes, but here in its first appearance the chorale is stated plainly. The words, however, are those of a different chorale, "Erkenne mich, mein huter": "Know me my keeper, my shepherd, take me to you. By you, the source of all good, much good has befallen me. Your mouth has refreshed me with milk and sweetmeats; your spirit has favored me with many a heavenly longing." Bach extends the metaphor of Jesus as shepherd, begun implicitly with the pastoral tone of "Ich will dir mein Herze schenken," and made clear in the words of the previous recitative.

The next recitative dramatizes the dialogue between Jesus and Peter in 26:33–35. Bach sets Peter's brave words promising never to abandon Jesus in firmly stated phrases; Jesus's knowing reply "Verily I say unto you that this night, before the cock crow, thou shalt deny me thrice" (26:34) Bach sets in sorrow, emphasized by the sighing of his string accompaniment. Another chorale to the melody of "Herzlich tut mich verlangen" follows; the words of "Ich will hier bei dir stehen" contrast bitterly with the dramatic situation: "I would stand here beside you; do not then scorn me! From you I will not depart, even if your heart is breaking. When your heart grows pale in death's final pang, then will I grasp you in my arms and lap." Peter and the other disciples will react with an all too human fear when named as disciples of Jesus, while the congregation of the faithful represented by the chorus cannot help Jesus in his suffering, despite their piety and good intentions.

Another recitative carries the narrative through verse 38, in which Jesus stops in the garden of Gethsemane to pray. The Evangelist's vocal line twists painfully as he relates how Jesus "began to be sorrowful and very heavy" (26:37), and the strings throb as Jesus sings that his "soul is exceeding sorrowful, even unto death," while his vocal line sinks low, and Bach shifts the harmony into a darker key to express Jesus's grief at this terrible moment.

The motivic accompagnato "O Schmerz!" (O sorrow!) and "Ich will bei meinem Jesu wachen" (I will watch beside my Jesus), the aria that follows, hit the highest point in the *St. Matthew Passion* yet after the opening chorus; they are stunning in their boldness and dimensions. Here, Bach deploys orchestral and choral forces far larger than in any previous aria or introductory passage. The tenor soloist is accompanied by two flutes and two oboi da caccia, the deeper-toned, obsolete woodwind, from the first orchestra, and the full second chorus, with two violins, a viola, and the continuo of the second orchestra. Both continuo sections underlie these carefully weighted vocal and instrumental groups, especially the winds. In scale and complexity, "O Schmerz!" and "Ich will bei meinem Jesu wachen" seem like the sum—and then some—of all the previous accompagnatos and arias.

What makes them sound so huge, in addition to the larger instrumental forces, are Bach's interweaving of a chorale with Henrici's devotional text. Moreover, Bach accords the chorale the freest treatment in these passages, linking its verses across the introduction and the aria, but breaking it up, altering it rhythmically and harmonically, orchestrating it elaborately, and widening its dimensions considerably, particularly at the end of the aria. This is not Bach's first attempt to fuse aria and chorale; he had broken that ground with two striking examples for bass and chorus in part II of the *St. John Passion*: "Eilt, ihr angefochtnen Seelen" (Hasten, you troubled souls) and "Mein theurer Heiland, lass dich fragen" (My dear Savior, let me ask you).

The motivic accompagnato opens with the tenor singing "O sorrow! Here trembles the anxious heart! How it sinks! How pales his face!" accompanied by the plangent flutes and oboes of the first orchestra over the anxious throbbing of the continuo. Bach's harmonies, shot through with delicate dissonance, are marvelously expressive of the words. His writing for the woodwinds is exquisite, but each instrumental line also exhibits a steely strength. Abruptly, the second chorus enters, singing "What is the cause of all these woes?" to the melody of "Herzliebster Jesu." The strings that accompany them are calmer than the winds, but the harmony is troubled.

The effect of the varied vocal, instrumental, melodic, and harmonic textures suddenly expanded, then crushed together, is shocking. The listener seems to hear a universal grief as the individuals and the muttering crowd state their emotions, varied in expression but alike in pious horror. The soloist continues his agonized lament: "The judge leads him to judgment; there is no comfort, no helper," emphasizing the words "judgment," "comfort," and "helper." Moving steadily on its own track, the chorus quietly replies, "Ah, my sins have felled you."

In greater agitation, the soloist sings, "He suffers all the pains of hell" (with a long, high note for "suffers"); "He must pay for others' robbery," the last two words emphasize. The chorus, to its quieter background of strings, comments: "Ah, Lord Jesus, I deserve this, that you are suffering." The tenor, backed by the winds, sings the last and most agitated lines of this extraordinary passage, "Ah, could my love for you, my Savior, diminish or help you bear your fear and trembling, how gladly would I remain with you." Here the tenor must reach for high notes and sing quicker notes, jumps, drops and other expressive ruptures of the vocal line, which the winds then imitate. For emphasis, Bach repeats the phrase "how gladly." These demands on the singer's range, agility, and expression make this line difficult to sing, and one of the most operatic in the *St. Matthew Passion*.

In "Ich will bei meinem Jesu wachen," the aria for tenor with choral interjections that follows, Bach keeps to the large aural canvas of the motivic accompagnato. But the aria's tone is calmer than the near frenzy of the introduction, and its pacing more spacious and broad. "I will watch beside my Jesus," the soloist sings; "Then our sins go to sleep," the chorus comments. "His soul's distress atones for my death; his mourning fills me with joy," the tenor continues. "So his meritorious Passion must be for us truly bitter, yet sweet" are the paradoxical closing words of the chorus.

The oboe, its tone at once sharp and sweet, opens the piece with a long but memorable tune, built, like many by Bach, of joined phrases. This one tends to jump bravely upward, then descend more gradually; leaps downward from high, followed by jumps most of the way back up, and then further down again (common in Bach's melodic vocabulary) form the final link in its long chain. The tenor sings the text to the instrumental melody almost note for note. The chorus's quiet ruminations to the tune of "Herzliebster Jesu" create an aural background to the tenor and oboe in front of this large-scale composition too big and elaborate to fit into the relatively simple da capo format. Instead, it is through-composed, meaning that Bach wrote out every note. It resembles a da capo piece in the way Bach uses the soloist's second line (*Meinem tod . . .*) as a middle section, switching also to a major key and longer, more reflective notes for the singer, followed by a lavishly decorated run on the word "freude" (joy). He then repeats the opening line.

Bach makes the final choral interjection longer and more elaborate than the previous ones, stretching this passage into a long, very beautiful dying fall that unforgettably captures the sensation of drifting off to sleep; the chorus repeats "schlafen" (sleep) five times over this thirteen-bar passage. His orchestration, using the flutes and strings of his second orchestra, is rich, and the rocking rhythm into which he breaks the chorale suggests that of a lullaby. Thus Bach, the shrewd dramatist, offers release from the tormented introduction in the peace of the concluding verses for the chorus. On a spiritual level, he supplies the tenor with music that is predominantly upright, sturdy, and hopeful, which contrasts with but also complements that of the chorus. That sublime element, ruled by the image of the peaceful sleep of the redeemed in this life and, more significantly, in death, is drenched with a rapturous surrender to sleep, the sleep of death, and to Christ for his divine self-sacrifice. In "O Schmerz!" and "Ich will bei meinem Jesu wachen," Bach contrasts a host of elements, textual and musical, concrete and implied, in his conception of this multidimensional music. The result satisfies intellect, emotion, and spirit.

The Evangelist resumes the narrative with a short recitative that covers the powerfully affecting verse 39 of Matthew 26. Frightened and sorrowful, Jesus falls down, praying, "If it be possible, let this cup pass from me: nevertheless not as I will, but as thou wilt." Bach lavishes care on even this tiny section, giving Jesus's prayer a plaintive tone. A motivic accompagnato for bass soloist follows. "The Savior falls down before his father," he sings, "thereby he raises me and all men from our fall upward to God's grace once more. He is ready to drink death's bitter cup, into which the sins of this world are poured, and stink foully, because it pleases dear God."

For the short but powerful motivic accompagnato that follows, Bach takes his cue from the double meanings of Henrici's text. A dark-toned viola joins the two violins that will accompany the aria this passage introduces, as the strings tumble sternly downward in fierce arpeggios which musically link Jesus's agonized fall to earth to pray with humanity's great fall from divine grace. The vocal line is deeply expressive, as well, with the heaviest emphases, as one would expect, on the words "fall," and "the cup."

Henrici's convoluted text for "Gerne will ich mich bequemen" (I will gladly submit), the compact da capo aria that follows, is a fine example of Pietist poetry. "I will gladly submit myself to take up the cross and cup, since I drink as the Savior did," the bass soloist sings. "For his mouth, which flows with milk and honey, has made the cause and the bitter shame of suffering sweet through his first draught." Bach steps back from the spaciousness of "Ich will bei meinem Jesu wachen" with his inward-looking treatment of the morbid lyric.

Just two violins and continuo set forth a winding, archaic, serious melody in a strange, limping dance rhythm, which the singer emulates. Like the longer melody of "Ich will bei meinem Jesu wachen," this difficult tune is a sequence of shorter components. Bach uses the expressive sigh of the half-step interval to set the key words, including "cross" and "cup," as well as the words that land at ends of lines. Bach breaks his rhythm frequently, creating some jarring syncopations, notably at the end of the opening section, by holding notes unexpectedly. In the "B" section— the middle section—the music drifts briefly into major, but its tone remains resolutely gloomy. Despite the imagery of sweetness in the libretto, there is nothing sweet about this tight, intense, black diamond of an aria.

The Evangelist picks up the narrative at 26:40 with a pained recitative in which Jesus finds his disciples asleep: "The spirit indeed is willing, but the flesh is weak," he comments sadly. Desperately, but without hope, Jesus prays once more to God that "if this cup may not pass away from me, except I drink it, thy will be done" (26:42). The chorus sings the chorale "Was mein Gott will, das g'sceh' allzeit" (What my God wills, may it ever be so), marking its only appearance in the *St. Matthew Passion*. "His will is the best; he is ready to help those who firmly believe in him," the text continues. "He helps in time of need and chastises in measure. He will not forsake him who trusts and builds firmly on him," is the essence of the words, which are sung to their traditional setting.

Judas's betrayal and the arrest of Jesus as related in 26:43–50 are the subject of the next recitative, terrible in its starkness. There is a rising figure for the first violin as Bach imagines Jesus raising his arm to wake the disciples and point to Judas and the approaching mob, but the betrayal itself is shockingly quick, done almost before the listener takes it in; the composer renders Jesus's mild rebuke, "Friend, wherefore art thou come?" (26:50) with the briefest melodic emphases, but otherwise just as plainly as the biblical text.

Here the *Passion* reaches its first dramatic crisis. The response of Bach and Henrici is a great, desolate, fairly well-known duet for the soprano and alto with chorus, "So ist mein Jesus nun gefangen" (So is my Jesus captured now), connected without pause with the turba chorus, "Sind Blitze, sind Donner" (Has lightning, has thunder), of colossal proportions and power. While reminiscent of the tenor's mold-breaking aria (also with chorus), "Ich will bei meinem Jesu wachen," heard only a few minutes earlier, this is freer formally, mixing aria and turba chorus. Its tone expresses none of the hope of earlier arias, but despair, grief, and rage in its place.

Bach opens the aria with a statement of the long melody in the winds, comprised of two halves, each half built of several phrases. Again and again, he exploits the weeping sound of the falling appoggiatura to make the sorrowful affect of the aria clear; the melody writhes and twists painfully over a string accompaniment that is in a more steady rhythm. But the overall effect is that of the voices stumbling like lost souls in near-total darkness. One of the most remarkable aspects of "So ist mein Jesus nun gefangen" is how small a sound Bach elicits—quite intentionally—from the full first orchestra (of the two orchestras, that is) of winds and strings. He does not, however, give the continuo a part, lightening the orchestral texture while amplifying the unmoored feeling of the music.

Once the singers enter, the weeping imagery becomes clearer as they play off each other in winding melismas that create many agonizing, dissonant clashes between their twining melodic lines. "So is my Jesus captured now," they sing, when the second chorus, backed by the second orchestra enters abruptly, with the words "Loose him! Stop! Bind him not!" Nothing could be more shocking or contrast more vividly with the wailing of the solo vocalists than these interjections, which Bach sets one harsh syllable to a note—there is hardly a more gripping and cathartic moment in all music than this, which in itself places the *St. Matthew Passion* firmly among the greatest works of musical drama.

Although behaving in a typical turba fashion, the chorus here, as in the big choral movement that follows, plays the role of the faithful, rather than its usual turba roles of bloodthirsty mobs, Jews, and soldiers. Here, of course, they cry out in helpless rage to those who have just arrested Jesus. The soloists' twining melodic lines continue: "Moon and light are quenched for sorrow because my Jesus is captured," they sing in parallel, their lines in a bleak harmony reminiscent of moaning. Again, the second chorus erupts in its mighty cry: "Loose him! Stop! Bind him not!" as the soprano and alto finish their line in coiling melismas. There is a third and final interjection from the chorus, representing Bach's audience of believers, before the soloists begin the final verse of the aria:

"They lead him, he is chained." The singers chant these six words three times, as though in appalled disbelief. Here they sing to steadier, rocking rhythm, often together, but the affect continues to be one of desolation and horror at man's mindless mistreatment of the instrument of his salvation.

Without an instant's pause, the bassos of both choruses 1 and 2, backed by the tonal weight and bite of their two continuo sections, tear into the turba chorus, "Sind Blitze, sind Donner" as Bach unleashes the tremendous pent-up emotion he has allowed to accumulate over the past hour of his titanic religious-musical drama but which the powerful choral interruptions of "So ist mein Jesu nun gefangen" cracked open. The bassos are quickly joined, in turn, by the tenors, altos, and sopranos in in Henrici's fierce and pithy lyrics: "Has lightning, has thunder vanished in the clouds? Open your fiery pit, o Hell, wreck, ruin, engulf, shatter with sudden force the false betrayer, the murderous blood."

As in the aria, the chorus takes the point of view of the Christian soul, here appalled and enraged by Judas's betrayal. The music hurtles ahead at a headlong speed (marked *vivace*—lively) which we have not heard before, even in the earlier turbae, but as in those choruses, the rhythm is unmistakably that of the dance. Many will be reminded of Vivaldi's concerto finales by the breakneck ferocity of the music, and they will be correct, for Bach admired the Italian's music greatly and learned much from him. Though not much longer than a minute and a half, the movement wields a far more powerful punch than its length suggests.

"Sind Blitze, sind Donner" contains many formal refinements worth listening for, once one gets somewhat used to its breathtaking power and drive. A few of these details include the brilliant writing for the flutes, which fly scattershot above the hurtling tide of the orchestras; the shocking full stop and pause for breath at the exact center of the movement and the startling change of key afterward; and the stunning writing for the choruses as they bark the imprecations "wreck, ruin, engulf, shatter" antiphonally at each other, an effect much enhanced in a live performance. Bach's masterful pacing on large and small scales is notable, as well. The way "So ist mein Jesus nun gefangen" leads directly into "Sind Blitze, sind Donner" lends a sense of freedom of form and mode of expression to the highly wrought work that is the *St. Matthew Passion*, and its place near the end of part I discharges much of the dark and bitter emotion accumulated by that point. By 1736, when Bach inserted the giant choral movement "O Mensch, bewein' dein' Sünde groß," the skilled artist in him realized that something more was called for as well.

But before that inspired addition there is one last recitative, which narrates the arrest of Jesus and the events surrounding it, as related in Matthew 26:51–56. This includes the incident in which Peter draws his sword and strikes off the ear of one of the high priest's servants. Jesus reproaches his hotheaded follower in firm tones, telling him that "all they that take the sword shall perish by the sword" (26:52). More sadly, he asks if they do not believe that he could pray to his Father, who would give him "more than twelve legions of angels? But how then shall the scriptures be fulfilled, that thus it must be?" (26:53–54). Jesus reproaches the arresting mob for manhandling him like a murderer (or a thief, in the King James translation), though he "sat daily with you teaching in the temple" (26:55), adding glumly again that all these events were predicted by the prophets. The Evangelist then sings the final, devastating narrative line of part I: "Then all the disciples forsook him, and fled" (26:56).

Bach's original ending for part I of the *St. Matthew Passion* was another "simple" chorale, "Meinen Jesum laß' ich nicht" (I shall not leave my Jesus). He had ended both parts of the *St. John Passion* with chorales, but in the nine years between the first performance of the *St. Matthew Passion* in 1727 and his reworking it into its "final" form in 1736, Bach came to feel that the scope of the work called for something greater in size and different in its expressive nature at this crucial moment in the drama and important juncture of this huge and complex musical structure. This led him to an act of inspired cannibalism, as he lifted the large-scale choral fantasy "O Mensch, bewein' dein' Sünde groß" from its place as the opening movement of the second version of the *St. John Passion* to its new position here.[24]

The long text of this chorale fits perfectly well at this point:

> O Man, bewail your great sin; for this, Christ, from his Father's bosom went forth and came to earth. Of a virgin pure and gentle he was born here for our sake; he was willing to mediate. He gave life to the dead, and conquered all sickness until the time came that he should be sacrificed for us, to carry the heavy burden of our sins upon the Cross itself."

Described by some writers as a fantasy, by others as an elaboration, "O Mensch, bewein" is a free treatment for the twin choruses and orchestras, as well as the high-

---

24. Wolff, *Johann Sebastian Bach*, p. 297.

soprano choir also used in the opening, all of which Bach unites here, on a chorale theme, somewhat resembling a theme and variations, in which the composer stays close at every moment to his source material. Keeping the theme—the chorale melody—chiefly in the possession of the choruses, Bach moves the accompaniments among the instrumental groups.

A score may prove helpful here, even for listeners who cannot read music: by following the words, and using a bit of instinct, one can at least see how Bach treats his theme. But in this movement, the figurations that decorate the chorale melody share center stage with the tune itself, at some points embellishing it with glittering ornamentation, at others enfolding it tenderly, and often doing both. Bach introduces the decorative elements first: the movement opens with delicately hammered figuration in the flutes and oboes, a combination of detached and melodic notes in the strings, then long notes in the oboes, all underpinned by the organ as continuo, often in pedal tones held for long stretches. The instrumental groups pass these around for quite a while—a good minute of a movement that runs for about six minutes in most modern recordings.

When the high sopranos and sopranos finally enter with the chorale melody, their treatment of the theme seems fairly plain compared to the busy activity of the instruments all around, and to the more ornate versions of the tune sung by the altos, tenors, and basses. There is always a lot going on, but first-timers should pay attention to how Bach keeps every element strictly relevant to the chorale melody. Bach's chorale preludes for organ, in which the composer takes a chorale theme as the basis for an instrumental fantasy that is nevertheless tightly structured, are close in form and spirit to "O Mensch, bewein," though necessarily smaller in scale.

For some listeners, however, "O Mensch, bewein" sounds unlike anything it follows in part I of the *St. Matthew Passion*; the sound and mood of the movement are indeed unlike anything in the oratorio. For others, the movement may feel remote and unsatisfying emotionally after the strong and poignant feelings evoked before. Grand as it is, the choral fantasy allows the listener to sit back, breathe deeply, and admire Bach's compositional virtuosity; the music remains relevant to the topic, but grants the listener a rest from the high emotion of all the previous moments of the *St. Matthew Passion* before the music presses on to its tragic outcome. "O Mensch, bewein" provides Bach with his only opportunity to vary the point of view of this long, intense work, serving formally like a digression in a long novel or epic poem.

Large in scope and in technical display, "O Mensch, bewein" also acts as a decorative counterpoise and response to "Kommt, ihr Töchter," the work's massive and affect-driven opening chorus. And finally, Bach must have realized that this impressive chorale fantasy adds more much-needed material to part I, which is still considerably shorter than the second part of the oratorio. The addition in 1736 of "O Mensch, bewein" represents the composer stepping back and looking at his canvas with the perspective of a decade, and shrewdly deciding that a big block in a cooler musical hue would help to balance his vast display of religious and dramatic expression.

Chapter 3

Part II

AS WITH MOST of the musical settings of the Passions, the Good Friday sermon—a major annual challenge for any Lutheran minister—was preached between parts I and II of the *St. Matthew Passion.* Assuming that Bach's performing tempos were brisk, like those favored today, the music would have run for two and three-quarter hours. Sermons were long, no less than thirty minutes, and other liturgical matters, including blessings, spoken prayers, and hymn singing might have added another good quarter-hour to a very long service. Bach made the presiding ministers' jobs unenviable, even impossible, on the two, three, or four Good Fridays when he led the *St. Matthew Passion*; even the most eloquent would have been swamped by the sheer volume—not to mention the devastating power and poignancy—of the music.

Part II of the *St. Matthew Passion* takes just over ninety minutes to perform, making it nearly half again as long as part I. Its narrative carries the story through Jesus's trial by Pontius Pilate, his scourging and mocking, and his crucifixion and entombment. Musically, the thirty-eight numbers of part II include nine arias (six preceded by motivic accompagnatos), eight chorales, and a concluding chorus of dimensions comparable to those that open and close part I. The remaining numbers consist of recitatives and turba choruses, which, because the narrative is more eventful, play a greater role than in part I, acting here as the connection between many of the other numbers. The cast of the "second act" is greater, too: in addition to every character in part I, Pontius Pilate, his wife, two maids, two false witnesses, and the high priest make contributions; Pilate's is the largest of the new solo parts.

In the crucial opening movement of part II, Bach places a beautiful, generously proportioned aria for alto with choral accompaniment to a text by Henrici. The structure of "Ach, nun ist mein Jesus hin" (Ah, my Jesus has gone now) is also highly sophisticated, consisting of a dialogue between the soloist and chorus that puts the listener in mind of the dialectic of "Kommt, ihr Töchter," the chorus that opens the work. But the aria's smaller scale, more personal tone, and grief-stricken affect, set the two movements apart, as does the delicacy of its musical expression, when set against the terrible power of "Kommt, ihr Töchter."

Henrici's verse summons the allegorical figures of the opening movement of the work, drawing connections and parallels, some explicitly, others more subtly. "Ah, my Jesus has gone now," the singer laments, to which the chorus replies, "Where then has your friend gone, O fairest among women?" The singer here serves not only as a faithful worshipper, but also as the community of faithful, symbolized as the Holy City of Jerusalem, which seeks its mate, the lost Savior. "Is it possible? Can I see it?" the alto asks, to which the chorus responds, "Where has your friend strayed?"—the "friend" being Jesus. "Ah, my Lamb in tiger's claws! Ah, where has my Jesus gone?" the soloist sings in horror, using another metaphorical name for Jesus. The chorus answers, comfortingly, "Then we will seek him with you." The soloist sings the aria's final line: "Ah! What shall I tell my soul when it asks me, full of fear? Ah, where has my Jesus gone?"

The composer takes his lead from Henrici, opening the aria with a long, typically Bachian melody, built of linked phrases in a delicate but clear dance rhythm, stated by a richly scored ensemble of flute, oboe d'amore, two violins, viola, and continuo from the first orchestra. Bach weaves the texture of soloist and chorus densely, as he did in the two arias with chorus in part I. The singer enters with a sustained, mournful note on the syllable "ach" as the instrumental group repeats the melody, then picking up the melody herself (or himself, when sung by a countertenor). The choral reply, accompanied by the violins and violas of the second orchestra, has a cool, consoling tone, as does their flowing response to the singer's devastated questioning "Is it possible? Can I see it?"

The setting of the line "Ah, my Lamb in tiger's claws!" is striking for the sharp rhythmic gestures Bach writes into the melody, depicting in their angularity the sharpness of the figurative "tiger's claws" themselves, as well as the affective despair of the faithful soul. The final line, repeating the opening, brings back the doleful note on "ach," and stops, rather than ends, on an open phrase that lacks a concluding cadence. Here as always, Bach follows Henrici's carefully, stopping the piece on the musical equivalent of the terrible question to which there is no comforting answer. From first note to last, "Ach, nun ist mein Jesus hin" is a magnificent display of Bach's profound attention to his libretto, and of his skill at writing music that clarifies, amplifies, and deepens its meaning.

A musically straightforward recitative picks up the story at Matthew 26:57. The Evangelist relates how Jesus was led to Caiaphas, the high priest, a fearful Peter following from afar. The priests, who have decided that Jesus must die, sought false witnesses to testify against the teacher, preacher, and prophet whose sole purpose is to uplift humanity, "yet found they none" (26:60). The first chorale of part II, "Mir hat die Welt trüglich gericht'" (The world has judged me deceitfully) follows. "The world has judged me deceitfully, with lies and false utterance," the chorus sings, "many a snare and secret plot." The closing line is a prayer: "Lord, guard me in this danger, shield me from false deceits." Sung to its regular melody, this is also one of the three chorale tunes heard only once in the *St. Matthew Passion*. By placing it at this moment in the drama, Bach and Henrici have embarked on a digression, in which they meditate on the role of false witnesses and lies in Jesus's entrapment, and more broadly on the prevalence of falsehood in this corrupt world, and the dangers of this particularly malicious sin.

In the recitative that follows, the priests of the temple have managed to come up with two false witnesses, as related in 26:60–63. Bach sets their lies ("This fellow said, I am able to destroy the temple of God and to build it in three days") tellingly, in twining, blustery lines supported by the busy motion of the continuo. The high priest asks Jesus for his reply, "but Jesus held his peace" (26:63). Bach rounds out the section on lies with "Geduld, Geduld" (Patience,

patience), the aria for tenor and the motivic accompagnato that leads into it. This stark aria is likely to be a tough nut for novices to crack, and the introductory passage, "Mein Jesus schweigt" (My Jesus holds his peace), is one of the more unusual of all the motivic accompagnatos in the *St. Matthew Passion* in its sound and affect.

"My Jesus holds his peace before false lies," the tenor soloist sings, "to show us that his merciful will is bent on suffering for our sake, and that, in similar pain, we should be like him, holding our peace in time of persecution." Bach accompanies Henrici's noble thought with a steady stream of detached chords for two oboes, the viola da gamba, and continuo that sounds almost like panting, creating an air of tense expectancy. According to scholar Alfred Dürr,[25] Bach added the viola da gamba to both the introduction and aria for a performance of the *Passion* in the 1740s when a different instrumental complement than he had scored the work for was available. The viola da gamba is a bass viol with frets on the neck, which the cello supplanted around the middle of the eighteenth century. The tone of the older instrument is at once far softer and more metallic, and its action sounds stiffer (though it is in fact smoother to play) than that of its more fluid, powerful successor. In any case, the sonority Bach achieves with oboes over crisply articulated chords for the strings is unusual in music from the Baroque era.

Most of the arias preceded by motivic accompagnatos continue with the instruments of the introduction. But here the oboes drop out, leaving the viola da gamba and continuo group as the tenor's lean accompaniment. "Patience,

---

25. J. S. Bach, *Matthäus-Passion* [St. Matthew Passion], ed. Alfred Dürr, p. ix.

patience," he sings, "even when false tongues sting me. Contrary to my guilt I suffer abuse and mockery: ah, then, may dear God avenge my heart's innocence." Bach's treatment for Henrici's crabbed, angry lyric (quite un-Christian in its vengefulness) is a two-part melody that reflects the repressed fury of the words. The first part, in even notes, accompanies the word "geduld" on every appearance but the final one. The second melodic cell is a series of what musicians call "dotted" notes, referring to the way it is notated. These notes are alternatingly short and long, with the long notes accented heavily: de *dumm*, de *dumm*, de *dumm*. This rhythm can suggest many emotions, but here they seem to depict vexation that is about to break into open rage. "Geduld"—patience—is repeated on the longer, even notes, with a tone that suggests a man exhorting himself to exercise that virtue while tempted beyond measure to lose his temper. Listen, too, to Bach's furiously brilliant settings of the German words "falsche" (false), "stechen" (sting), "Schimpf" (abuse), and "Spott" (mockery).

Without doubt, "Geduld, Geduld" is a masterpiece of psychological description in music. But its lean, tough sonority and stiff gait make it more difficult to enjoy in the way one might bask in the rich sound of the preceding aria "Ach, nun ist mein Jesu hin," or relish the beauties of the grandest solo in the work, "Erbarme dich," which soon follows. The key to appreciating "Geduld, Geduld" is to pay close attention to the care and wit that Bach, known for his own hot-tempered impatience, lavishes on every word.

Moving quickly, the next four numbers in the score cover much ground: Matthew 26:63–75, in which the high priest Caiaphas questions Jesus, and Peter, who has approached as closely as he dares, is recognized as one of the disciples. The first of these movements is a recitative covering verses 63 to 66, in which the high priest asks Jesus whether he claims to be "Christ, the Son of God" (63), to which the Savior again uses his unforgettable affirmation, "Thou sayest," adding a majestic, billowing figure for the violins to Jesus's string accompaniment as he says, "Hereafter shall ye see the Son of Man sitting on the right hand of power, and coming in the clouds of heaven" (64). In a rage that is at least partly for show—this is, after all, what Caiaphas hoped Jesus would say—the priest "rent his clothes, saying, 'He hath spoken blasphemy; what further need have we of witnesses?'" (65). Calling to the crowd, he asks "what think you?" A rushing figure in the bass leads without pause into the short (five bars) turba chorus in both choruses and orchestras portraying the mob, eager for blood, answering in a jagged melodic pattern: "He is guilty of death" (66). Here Bach employs a *fugato*, a kind of writing that sounds like a fugue in its close entries of the different parts, but is not a fully developed fugal structure. The effect is of the members of the crowd crying out in anger, but randomly.

In a short recitative, the Evangelist relates how "They did spit in his face, and buffeted him; and others smote him with the palms of their hands (67). As before, this leads directly into a *turba* portraying the mockery of Jesus by the mob. Again, Bach's fugato writing for the choruses and orchestras effectively captures the wild nature of the crowd, organizing its chaos into tightly controlled lines; but here the movement is longer, allowing the composer to delineate a more complete dance rhythm than in the previous, very brief *turba* movement. It is hard once again not to hear Bach's admiration for Vivaldi in this concertolike movement, in which the mob sings so cruelly, and with such bitter irony, "Prophesy unto us, thou Christ, Who is he that smote thee?" (68).

The chorale "Wer hat dich so geschlagen" (Who has buffeted you so), sung to the "O Welt, ich muss dich lassen" melody provides a brief moment of respite as the drama rushes ahead. "Who has buffeted you so, my Salvation, and with torments used you so harshly? You are, indeed, no sinner, like us and our children; of misdeeds you know nothing," is the text of this hymn. Here and there rhythmic pulls, as well as slips in the harmony, suggest the heavy sorrow the situation must evoke in the faithful listener, but overall the chorale allows for a moment of cooler reflection as the tragedy presses forward.

Peter's betrayal, which Jesus prophesied in detail, is played out powerfully in the recitative with a turba at its center that follows. Following 26:69, the Evangelist relates how two young women recognized Peter as a disciple of Jesus, which he denies three times, "cursing and swearing" (74) that he is not one of Jesus's group. The crowd (in *turba*) breaks in, "Surely thou art one of them, for thy speech bewrayeth [betrays] thee" (73), but Peter continues his denials. The cock crows, the Evangelist sings, mimicking the bird's call with his vocal line; Peter recalls Jesus's words, "and he went out, and wept bitterly" (75). Here, Bach's emotional, dramatic, and spiritual trajectories meet in "Erbarme dich" (Have mercy), the grand confessional aria for alto.

If the *St. Matthew Passion* were an opera, this would be the moment in the libretto when one of the main characters is in an intolerable situation. This type of scenario is one of the chief purposes of dramatic music, for the composer is now free to unleash a flood of melody—heartfelt rather than passionate—that leaves the audience bathed in tears. (Handel was one of the greatest masters of this kind of aria; even those who are well acquainted with "Lascia ch'io piangi"—Leave me to weep—from *Rinaldo* find themselves predictably in or near tears every time they hear the simple, infinitely moving tune.) The dramatic situation of Jesus abandoned by his followers and Peter weeping for his own weakness allows Bach to unleash "Erbarme dich" on an audience itself ready to weep. Henrici's direct, moving words do not create a maze of overwrought Pietist imagery; instead they offer the composer a direct path to the expression of spiritual grief. One can imagine Bach telling his librettist, "Keep this simple!"

"Have mercy, my God, for my tears' sake; look here: heart and eyes weep bitterly before you. Have mercy!" These are the lyrics of this most beautiful, touching, and comprehensible aria, for many listeners the very heart of the *St. Matthew Passion*, in the direct outpouring of contrition to God by the faithful but troubled soul. In their plainness they stand just a step behind *Kyrie eleison* (Lord, have mercy on us), the devastatingly simple Greek prayer in the Catholic liturgy, in which the congregation assumes the role of mankind, all acting as one. "Erbarme dich" takes an individual's point of view, carrying with it the implications of humanity: here, one speaks eloquently for all. In both texts, less is more, as ultimately there is little for the faithful soul to say apart from these few potent words begging for God's mercy.

Given the seriousness of the lyrics, the first-time listener to "Erbarme dich" may well be surprised by the lightness of the music, a lilting duet for alto voice and solo violin, set against the delicate veil of sound created by two violins and a viola, all underpinned by the continuo instruments (cello, double bass and organ). These two deep-toned strings are plucked (*pizzicato*) throughout the movement, further lightening its texture, and adding an unforgettable twilit beauty to its sound.

The solo violin introduces the long, drooping melody, which floats with infinite grace and an emotion beyond melancholy over the steady throb of the continuo. The rhythm is the same pastoral 12/8 Bach employed to very different effect in "Kommt, ihr Töchter," the opening chorus, with the massive swaying motion of that movement brought down here to a lyrical, dancelike beat more typical of music in this time signature. It also carries with it the same religious and metaphorical implications of the pastorale, with which attentive listeners should by now be somewhat familiar. Despite the sorrowful pitch of the music, there is something soothing in the familiar, easy rhythm, and Bach's long-breathed, even melodic, phrases offer comfort as well. "Erbarme dich" speaks directly to the heart, but in complex ways.

Bach sets the aria in three broad sections, using "Look here, heart and eyes weep bitterly before You" as the middle, but never disturbs the music's magical flow or its transparent instrumental and vocal textures. Listeners should pay attention to the way the violin takes the lead throughout the movement, decorating the melody with its weeping descant, although never overembellishing it—or the words when accompanying the singer—in a flurry of busy grace notes. Bach elaborates the singer's part only minimally;

sometimes the vocal line surges upward as though in pain, but often it lies low in the singer's range, sounding almost murmured. The words "mein Gott," which Bach distributes four times over the breadth of the aria's ample structure, are always sung one note to a syllable, as though uttered under the breath, and are elaborated only once, discreetly, on their final appearance. Despite the considerable skill Bach requires of both singer and solo violinist, the overall effect is as sincere and unshowy as one could imagine. For this very personal confession, standing at the heart of the *St. Matthew Passion*, Bach created a mood of rare intimacy, as though we are eavesdropping on an individual soul's newfound recognition of sin.

Bach, ever the astute dramatist, realized how magical a musical web he had spun with "Erbarme dich." Before plunging back into tragic narrative, he allows us to pause for a moment with the chorale "Bin ich gleich von dir gewichen." "Although I have strayed from you, yet have I returned again," the choruses sing. "Your son has reconciled us through his agony and mortal pain. I do not deny my guilt, but your grace and favor are greater than the sin which I always confess." This beautiful chorale, third and last of those sung only once in the *St. Matthew Passion*, opens in a halting, almost shell-shocked tone, gathering strength and confidence as it proceeds. It is perfectly suited to Bach's wish to ease the return after "Erbarme dich" to the Passion story.

The Evangelist resumes the narrative with the first verse of Matthew 27. The high priest and elders meet in the morning to seal Jesus's fate, delivering him to Pontius Pilate, the Roman governor of Palestine. Regretting his betrayal, Judas seeks to return the thirty pieces of silver: "I have sinned in that I have betrayed the innocent blood," says this most despised figure in his final line. In a quick *turba*, the priests can practically be heard turning away from Judas, calling in contempt to the now useless man, "What is that to us? See thou to that" (27:4). The Evangelist relates how Judas threw the money into the Temple, then ran off and hanged himself. Debating what to do with the money in a blusterous but compressed duet, with echoes persisting as late as the quarreling Jews of Richard Strauss's opera *Salome* of 1905, the priests agree that the tainted money must not be put back into the treasury of the Temple.

"Gebt mir meinen Jesum wieder!" (Give me back my Jesus), the brilliant aria for bass that follows is utterly oper-atic in its scale and affect. "Give me back my Jesus," rages the singer. "See, the money, the price of murder, the lost son throws at you, down at your feet." Bach's stunning musical trope for this long but fast-moving aria is the silvery solo for violin, which suggests the jingle of Judas's coins. The instru-mental ensemble is identical to that of "Erbarme dich," but the tough, bright sonority Bach elicits could not be more different. Gone are the long, graceful phrases of the previous aria, which are replaced here by chunky chords and unisons, rendered at a brisk pace. The aria's short-winded, stormy theme ends with a breathless pause; the mood of furious contempt for the traitor and his money could not be clearer. The vocal part is difficult, filled with runs, jumps and breaks in rhythm; the difficulty and brilliance of the violin part is equal to, and reminiscent of, a concerto solo. In keeping with the tone of the movement, the closing measure is an abrupt gesture.

A long sequence of recitatives, interspersed with turbae and chorales carries the narrative ahead, resuming at 27:6. In an interesting sidelight, the Evangelist relates how the priests bought with the thirty pieces of silver a "potter's field, to bury strangers in. Wherefore that field was called, The field of blood unto this day" (26:7–8). Of course, "potter's field" would become the generic name for municipal burial grounds for the indigent. Returning to the narrative, the Evangelist continues with Jesus's questioning by Pilate, a ruler struggling to act justly, but far more concerned with keeping peace, obviously an impossible task in first century Palestine. In reply to the governor's question "Art thou the King of the Jews?" Jesus, accompanied by the usual strings, gives his somewhat mysterious reply, "Thou sayest" (in essence, "you said it"). Pilate asks how Jesus responds to the accusations of the priests and elders, but Jesus remains silent "insomuch that the governor marvelled greatly" (27:14).

Here Bach inserts the chorale "Befiehl du deine Wege": "Commend your way, and whatever troubles your heart, to the care of him, who rules the heavens; he who gives clouds, air and winds the paths, course, and track: he will also find ways where your feet can walk." This Bach sets to the sad but consoling melody of "Herzlich tut mich verlangen." A densely packed, rapid recitative covering verses 15 to 22 follows. In this section, the Evangelist tells how, as a goodwill gesture for Passover, Pilate is forced by the mob to release the thief Barabbas instead of Jesus, whom he correctly views as a righteous man and a victim of the priests' plotting. In a believable detail, Pilate's wife sends word that Jesus, "that just man," should be released, "for

I have suffered many things this day in a dream because of him" (27:19).

But the mob, incited by the priests, howls fearfully for Barabbas. Bach renders its cry of his name concisely and with devastating force to the most basic dissonant chord in every composer's expressive vocabulary (a diminished seventh) This single interruption, included strictly for narrative purpose, is nevertheless searing in its dramatic power.

"What shall I do with then with Jesus?" Pilate asks the crowd. Its reply, "Let him be crucified!" is rendered in furious turba fashion. Bach subjects its aggressive fugue theme with a sharp Vivaldian profile to a dense series of entries by the chorus, but breaks it off sharply for a short chorale, "Wie wunderbarlich ist doch diese Strafe," to the "Herzliebster Jesu" chorale melody. "How wondrous is this punishment!" the chorus marvels, in hushed tones, "The good shepherd suffers for his sheep; the righteous master pays the penalty for his vassals!" Here of course the metaphors are thick, but the calm of the chorale contrasts powerfully with the rhythmic and melodic bite of the turba; so closely does Bach place them that they seem almost welded by a magnetic opposition.

Now Bach and Henrici split the atom, making remarkable use—structural, expressive, and philosophical—of the first phrase of Matthew 27:23, "And the governor said, Why, What evil hath he done?" turning the question into a lead-in for the motivic accompagnato that follows in answer. This interruption of the narrative in midverse to insert a big recitative and devotional aria is a fine demonstration of the careful thought that went into the design of the *St. Matthew Passion*, where nothing is ill-considered, unconsidered, or formulaic. This intense sequence may be viewed as the spiritual heart of the oratorio.

The soprano, backed by two oboi da caccia (the deeper-pitched Baroque cousin of the modern oboe that played an important role in the ensemble for the motivic accompagnato "O Schmerz!" in part I) answers,

> He has done good to us all. He gave sight to the blind, made the lame walk; he spoke his father's word, and drove the devils out; he raised up the afflicted, received and gave shelter to sinners. Nothing else has my Jesus done.

Bach entwines Henrici's verse amid the curling lines of the pair of winds, using the continuo to punctuate from below in detached notes that rise and fall between every line of text. A flute joins the oboes and the singer for "Aus Liebe will mein Heiland sterben" (Out of love my Savior is willing to die). The continuo, unusually, remains silent. Made only of three winds and one voice, without the deep tones of the continuo instruments or the bite of even a single string, the sound of this eloquent movement seems detached from the world, a creation of pure spirit.

The oboi da caccia play exquisitely slow staccato chords, as the flute chants a twisting, pain-filled melody above, which stops from time to time, then struggles back into motion with the gravity of thought itself. "Out of love my Savior is willing to die," the soprano meditates, with Bach stretching the last word out in wondrous languor, "though he knows nothing of any sin, so that eternal ruin and the punishment of judgment may not rest on his soul." Again and again, Bach draws out the words "love," "eternal," and, above all, "die" to heavenly lengths. The winds sing in voluptuously close harmony in this intense, dreamlike reflection, in which the composer grandly defies normal concepts of musical motion. This remarkable aria demands close, careful listening on its own terms; the impatient and restless stand no chance of grasping the profound expression of its messages and meanings.

Picking up the narrative in the middle of Matthew 27:23, where the composer and librettist paused to insert an aria, the Evangelist describes how "they [the mob] cried out the more, saying, Let him be crucified." Bach has both choruses and orchestras repeat the short fugal turba sung to the same words before the intervening chorale, motivic accompagnato, and the aria "Aus Liebe will mein Heiland sterben." But he sets the second iteration in a different key (B minor) pitched a tone above the earlier one, and which the ear therefore perceives as more fierce and intense, whether that ear belongs to a listener who knows about musical keys.

Seeing that he cannot rescue Jesus from the wrath of the mob without risking his fragile political stability, Pilate finally yeilds. In recitative, the Evangelist relates the famous story of the governor, who in a fine, dramatic gesture, actually washes his hands "before the multitude, saying, I am innocent of the blood of this just person: see ye to it" (27:24); this is the origin of the expression "I wash my hands of it." In a turba of greater dimension than the two very short ones to which "Let him be crucified" is set, the mob answers, in a reply that will ring grievously for Jews across the centuries, "His blood be on us, and our children" (27:25). A fugato movement like the two before, it is built of a theme that seems to sprout from the sharp-edged *Laß ihn kreuzigen* subject. Fierce, loud, and aggressive, this turba does not make pleasant or enjoyable listening, although one may ultimately appreciate the skill with which Bach made it. The Evangelist continues with Pilate's reluctant release of Barabbas; next, and worse, "when he had scourged Jesus, he delivered him to be crucified" (27:26).

"Können Tränen meiner Wangen" (If the tears on my cheeks), the majestic devotional aria for alto that follows, stands as another lofty peak in this great score. Bach precedes it with a motivic accompagnato that complements the aria and prepares the way for it. "Have mercy, God!" cries the alto. "Here stands the Savior, bound. O scourging, blows, wounds! Stop, you tormentors! Does the pain of your souls not soften you, nor the sight of such grief? Yes, your heart must be like a whipping post, or harder still. Have mercy, stop!"

Bach subjects Henrici's declamatory text to startling figurative treatment. Violins and violas repeat again and again a lashing figure in a long-short (dotted) pattern that depicts the blows of the whips scourging Jesus. This remarkable movement shows Bach's capability of executing tone-painting, the musical art of depiction, at the highest level. Faced with the same task, a lesser imagination might well yield to tastelessness. Instead, Bach suggests the horror of the event with the relentless application of strings, in their cutting tone, to the sharp slashing figure; and he sets Henrici's words, which demand dramatic treatment, in a highly pictorial manner that suits them perfectly.

In the sweep of the falling phrase that opens "Können Tränen," Bach extends and broadens the sharply accented rhythm of the preceding passage into a figure of gravity and depth; the second portion of the melody moves in a more singable, stepwise melodic pattern that ends somewhat unexpectedly on a high note. The two-part melody comprises all the thematic material of this magnificent da capo aria, sung by the alto accompanied only by violins and continuo. The contained form and small ensemble do not make the composer think small: "Können Tränen" is a movement of intensity, profundity, breadth, and power. "If the tears on my cheeks achieve nothing, ah, then take my heart," the singer addresses God in Henrici's highly symbolic verse. "But let it for the streams, when the wounds bleed gently, also be the sacrificial cup." Once we consider the meaning of the words, the grandeur of Bach's falling figure becomes obvious: he is painting in tone the initial image of the falling tears of the faithful, which connects with the image of the blood streaming from Jesus's wounds, provoking those pious tears.

The huge, almost grandiose figure of the opening phrase for the instruments outlines the chord of G minor, rather than the smaller, tighter intervals of "Erbarm' es Gott," the introductory motivic accompagnato; the second phrase moves at a stately pace, while the melody is in itself ineffably heart-easing. Bach never assigns the singer the big falling phrase, which he keeps as the chief metaphor and motto of the movement. That is always the tears, transformed to blood (akin perhaps to the transformations of the Eucharist), on which the faithful soul must brood. The singer's entrance, on a falling version of the warmer melodic phrase, sounds much like weeping, another aural image Bach extends through the movement. The middle of the "A" section (itself in three subgroups) turns to a consoling major key; after a breathless pause, the singer repeats the opening words to a coiling line of mounting intensity, chanting, "Ah, then take my heart" four times in seven bars. In the "B" section, Bach moves freely among several keys to great expressive effect, but the gravely exalted mood and the singular focus of this extraordinary aria remain unbroken.

The narrative resumes with the mocking of Jesus (Matthew 27:27-30). The Evangelist recounts how

> the soldiers of the governor . . . stripped him, and put on him a scarlet robe. And when they had platted [woven] a crown of thorns, they put it on his head, and a reed in his right hand: and they bowed the knee before him and mocked him, saying, Hail, King of the Jews! And they spit upon him, and took the reed, and smote him on the head."

Here Bach weaves a big, if brief, turba in which both choruses and orchestras sing the soldiers' mocking words into the Evangelist's sober narration, where the composer emphasizes the crown of thorns, the spitting, and the striking of the Savior with expressive chords for the continuo and high notes for the Evangelist to sing.

Now Bach inserts a long, memorable chorale, "O Haupt voll Blut und Wunden" (O head, bloody and wounded), to the "Herzlich tut mich verlangen" melody. At roughly double (or more) the performance time of the other chorales, "O Haupt voll Blut und Wunden" derives its length from its eight verses; most of the others have only four. The text, which takes Jesus's wounds as its point of meditative departure, is notable for its Pietist morbidity: "O head, bloody and wounded, full of pain and scorn, O head, wreathed for mockery with a crown of thorns! O head, once gorgeously adorned with highest honor and renown, but now highly abused: I greet you!" The concluding four verses present a tangle of images and rhetoric that are hard to translate: "Your noble face, before which the great Last Judgment shrinks and cowers, how it us spat upon! How pale you look: who has treated your eyes, which no light can equal, so shamefully amiss?" Bach's harmonization of this complex text is nevertheless fairly straightforward.

The Evangelist's subsequent recitative recounts how the soldiers remove the doubly ironic "royal" robe they put on Jesus to mock him, return his own garment to him, then "lead him away to crucify him" (27:31). Bach gives the key word a highly expressive, sensitive, falling harmony that sets it utterly apart from the rest of the recitative, which concludes with the story of the soldiers compelling a bystander, Simon of Cyrene, to carry the cross. Preparing the way for the paradox contained in the next devotional aria, "Komm, süßes Kreuz" (Come, sweet cross), Bach twists the Evangelist's vocal line upward, so that he ends with the final words *sein Kreuz trug* (his cross bear) on difficult high notes. The Evangelist's part continues to be painfully expressive from here to the end.

The Pietist paradox on which Bach and Henrici construct "Komm, süsses Kreuz" is based on the good fortune of Simon the Cyrene in carrying Jesus's cross, which awful task the faithful Christian soul should envy and undertake symbolically and in spirit. Preceding this difficult aria for bass and viola da gamba is the shortest motivic accompagnato in the *St. Matthew Passion*, only six bars long and just over thirty seconds in duration. "Yes, gladly are our flesh and blood compelled to the Cross," the soloist sings over rippling arpeggios for the gamba accompanied by a pair of soaring, ecstatic flutes; "it helps our souls the heavier it weighs."

Listeners who have heard Bach's sonatas and partitas for solo violin and, even more pertinent, the suites for solo cello, may recognize in "Komm, süsses Kreuz" a cousin to these extraordinary works; here too, the viola da gamba, backed by the continuo and covered by the bass, suggests full counterpoint without the means to play out every voice. Mind over matter, the ability of the ear to hear implied notes, as well as that of the player to master these difficult, but infinitely noble works, are all keys to Bach's music for the solo strings. Here, too, the small ensemble seems to struggle audibly with the idea of expressing acceptance of responsibility for one's own sin: "Come, sweet Cross, I will say, then: my Jesus, give it always to me. Should my pain become too heavy, then [you] help me to carry it myself." "Komm, süsses Kreuz" also resembles "Geduld, Geduld," the other aria for tenor and gamba, in its sense of effort.

As in "Geduld, Geduld," the gamba sets the tone in a stark "dotted" rhythm that marks this tough aria as well. In through-composed form, "Komm, süsses Kreuz" bears close resemblance to a da capo aria, with a middle section that shifts into a major key, and the closing section brings back the opening in varied form. Bach assigns long, twisting lines to the solo gamba, which the singer must copy, particularly on the word "Leiden" (pain)." Thus it seems Bach's affect of choice for "Komm, süsses Kreuz" is that of struggling, limping difficulty and pain of body and spirit. As in "Gerne will ich mich bequemen" for bass and violins in part I, the faithful must find sweetness in the bitterness of Jesus's suffering. Like that aria, "Komm, süsses Kreuz" seems anything but sweet, and is a good example of the masochistic side of some Pietist devotion which some modern listeners may find strange, and even incomprehensible.

The tragedy reaches its climax in the next complex sequence of recitative and turbae choruses. Resuming the story at 27:33, the Evangelist sings that Jesus was brought to Golgotha, which means "the place of the skull." The Aramaic place name—infamous yet rich with mystical reverberations as the place of the divine sacrifice—is sung on a high note, while the German translation echoes it at a lower pitch. The soldiers give Jesus "vinegar to drink mingled with gall"—a bitter cup, indeed—but which Jesus refuses after tasting. In the next line he is crucified, and his garments taken and divided, also fulfilling a prophecy. This awful material Bach sets to recitative that is plain, if filled with pain. The sign reading "This is Jesus the King of the Jews" is set above his head (27:37). The Evangelist tells of the two thieves cruci-fied with Jesus, one on either side. The Evangelist's next line, "And they that passed by reviled him, wagging their heads, and saying" leads directly into a long turba chorus, divided into two sections by a brief line of narrative.

"Thou that destroyest the temple, and buildest it in three days, save thyself," the mob calls, mocking him with the words of the false witnesses; "If thou be the Son of God, come down from the cross." Continuing the narrative with 27:41, the Evangelist sings that "likewise also the chief priests mocking him, with the scribes and elders, said"—here the chorus resumes "He saved others; himself he can-not save. If he be the King of Israel, let him now come down from the cross, and we will believe him. He trusted in God; let him deliver him now, if he will have him: for he said, I am the Son of God."

Bach opens this gripping movement, laid out for the two choruses and orchestras in an angry burst of dancelike figuration, which soon shifts into a more contrapuntal mode with the words "help yourself," and pulls itself to a furious half-stop on "cross." The continuation of the chorus following the Evangelist's brief line is longer and yet more powerful, but constructed in similar fashion. The dancelike opening ends on an angry pause before the fugato, in which the polyphony is thick yet quite free; some of the melodic lines are marked by snarling trills and some big unison gestures, as the composer drives the chorus toward its climax on the final line, its meanings, doubly ironic to the faithful, made crystal clear by a fierce underlining of every note: in their mockery, the priests unwittingly state the truth: Jesus *is* God's son. A tiny recitative for the Evangelist, in which he relates that the thieves crucified with Jesus "cast the same in his teeth" (27:44) rounds out the section.

"Sehet, Jesus hat die Hand" (See, Jesus had his hand), the bold, beautiful aria for alto with choral interjections follows. Bach precedes it, however, with a motivic accompagnato of considerable dimension and depth. Henrici's text is complex in language and heavy with paradox. "Ah, Gologotha, unhappy Golgotha!" the singer exclaims. "The Lord of Glory must perish wretchedly here; the world's blessing and salvation placed, like a curse, on the cross. From the Creator of heaven and earth, earth and air are taken away"—the librettist merges the divine Father and Son in the imagery of this somewhat confusing line—"The guiltless must die here, guilty. That strikes deeply into my soul. Ah, Golgotha, unhappy Golgotha!"

Bach's strangely beautiful setting matches the inward-
ness of the text. Two oboi da caccia, the chief instruments
of the aria to follow, move together at a stately pace in
close harmony; their twisting line seems more figuration
than melody, with long notes alternating with three quicker
ones. One of the most interesting and unusual aspects
of the movement is Bach's treatment of the continuo, in
which the cellos play a graceful, arching plucked figure
over longer-held deep notes for the organ and contrabass,
which is bowed. Over this dense and complex instrumental
pattern, the alto must perform jumps from high to low and
back again in tortured, heavily ornamented intervals. The
feeling of the music is close, even oppressive, in this difficult movement, which is also one of the most daring in
the score from a harmonic standpoint.

After the gloom and tension of the previous minutes, the
broad opening of "Sehet, Jesu hat die Hand" comes like a
hopeful gust of fresh air or a ray of light. Notable at once
is the wide-stepping movement of the continuo group,
normally quite contained, as it ascends swiftly and steeply,
while the two oboes burble ecstatically above. The magical sound of the aria is built chiefly of these two elements,
which the alto and second chorus soon join, keeping the
sound of this music grandly structured but diaphanous,
light, and open. Henrici's touching metaphor is of the crucified Christ extending his hands in an embrace of love and
pity for mankind. "See, Jesus had his hand stretched out to
grasp us: come!" the alto sings, to which the chorus, backed
very lightly by the second orchestra replies, each time with
one light note to a syllable: "Where?" "In Jesus's arms seek
redemption find mercy. Seek!" "Where?" the chorus asks,

with infinitely delicate hopefulness. "In Jesus's arms live, die, rest, you forsaken chickens, stay" is the soloist's reply, whereby Henrici deprives mankind of even the minimal dignity of comparison with sheep. "Where?" the chorus gently asks, one last time; "In Jesus's arms."

Baroque operatic styles seem to have little bearing on this wonderful concerted piece, in which Bach gives us a moment of relief that could not be more welcome at this most terrible moment in Jesus's tragic drama. First-time listeners should pay attention to the alto's manifest joy in summoning mankind to come, and her (or his) freely flowing vocal line in which the words "see," "stay," and even "die" roll fluidly from the singer's throat.

But the relief Bach offers is only momentary: the next four numbers in the score portray Jesus's last words, the final mocking cries of the crowd witnessing his crucifixion, and his death. Bach subjects these events to extreme compression, taking just over two pages in the full orchestral score; and it is here that the composer offers more music that is daring, and even radical.

As the Evangelist resumes the biblical narrative at 27:45, telling of the "darkness over the land from the sixth to ninth hour," Bach darkens the vocal line; when the Savior cries out in tormented Aramaic "Eli, Eli, lama sabachthani? That is to say, My God, my God, why hast thou forsaken me?" Bach withdraws the "halo" of Jesus's usual string accompaniment for this, the Savior's final and most human moment. The composer also inserts a tempo marking, *adagio*— slowly—rare in this or any of his scores, written in an era when performers inferred tempos based on the nature of the music. The Evangelist, rendering Jesus's Aramaic words into

German, mimics the notes sung by Jesus, but in a deeper, darker key (E-flat minor, rarely used before the nineteenth century) that colors the music and text yet more somberly. The crowd, watching Jesus's agonized death for its amusement, calls out in a tiny *turba* of one and one-half bars: "This man calleth for Elias." But one man among the pitiless mob dips a sponge into vinegar, raising it on the tip of a pole to give the dying man a bit of comfort. Again, the mob, implacable in its need to mock, yells: "Let be, let us see whether Elias will come to save him" in another short, harsh turba. "Jesus, when he had cried again with a loud voice, yielded up the ghost" (27:50). Bach sets the German word "verschied" (yielded), simply, but on a plangent, falling interval.

The hero of the divine tragedy is dead; what is left from a dramatic standpoint is to bring him to his rest. But a moment of prayer and reflection is first called for. Here Bach inserts "Wenn ich einmal soll scheiden" (When once I must depart), the final chorale of the oratorio, and the most remarkable. Bach sets this to the "Herzlich tut mich verlangen" melody, altering the music to follow the terror expressed in the words. The opening couplet, "When once I must depart, do not depart from me! When I must suffer death, then stand thou by me!" the choruses implore Jesus directly with heavy heart. With the next verse, "When I most full of fear at heart shall be," the melodic line sung by the bassos begins to slip downward in depression and terror; the composer has begun to pull away from the opening key of A minor. With the closing line, "Then snatch me from the terrors of fear and pain by thy strength" Bach tears the harmony from its root completely: we seem to be looking death in the eye. The conclusion droops down more (into E major), disturbing the reliably stable form of the chorale, making this one sound as though it has not ended, but slid away instead, in one of the most daring and alarming moments in this bold score.

Bach sets to music of dramatic splendor the apocalyptic events related in verses 51 through 54, which follow. The Evangelist sings in powerful, grandiose tones of the spontaneous tearing of the veil in the temple, the earthquakes, and the opening of the graves, disgorging "saints . . . [who] went into the holy city and appeared to many." Bach renders the trembling of the ground in shuddering fast notes for the contrabass, which are capable of terrifying even listeners who have heard the episode many times. The awestruck words of the Roman captain and soldiers officiating at the crucifixion, who "saw the earthquake, and those things that were done . . . feared greatly, saying, Truly, this was the Son of God" (27:54) are sung to a turba of a different character, slow and stunned, without the dancelike drive of the others. The story of how Joseph of Arimathea, the pious "rich man . . . who also himself was Jesus's disciple," (27:57) asks for and receives the body of Jesus from Pontius Pilate is told in the next recitative.

"Mache dich, mein Herze" (Make yourself, my heart), the next aria, and "Am Abend" (In the evening), the motivic accompagnato that introduces it, are the last of their kind in the *St. Matthew Passion*. This pair of devotional movements continues with the point of view which Bach and Henrici introduced in "Sehet, Jesus hat die Hand," in which the faithful soul expresses relief and gratitude for Jesus's sacrifice. This is not the final mood of the work, however; the narrative, which ends with Jesus's entombment, still must be concluded, and there are two final, grand meditations on the Savior's well-deserved rest after his earthly suffering is over. Each of these has its own distinct devotional posture and mode of expression.

Henrici's concept for the introductory passage takes the idea of a changed world on the evening after the crucifixion, a moment after which nothing could be as it was before, tying Jesus's sacrifice that day specifically with the Fall of Adam, referring also to the corrupt world cleansed by God with the great flood of Genesis 5–9, Noah's flood. Henrici's language is perhaps a bit morbid and convoluted for listeners of the twenty-first century, but his idea is well conceived. "In the evening, when it was cool, Adam's fall was manifest," the bass soloist sings, "In the evening, the Redeemer casts him [Adam] down; in the evening the dove returned, carrying an olive leaf in its mouth. O lovely moment! O evening hour! Peace is now made with God, for Jesus has endured his Cross. His body comes to rest. Ah, dear soul, I pray you go, bid them give you the dead Jesus. O wholesome, o precious keepsake!"

Bach's setting is a masterpiece of smoky, almost cinematic atmosphere. Moving in a steady pattern of even notes, the first violins keep toward the lower end of their range, while the second violins and violas support them with a stream of notes (all from orchestra 1), which move at half the speed of the first violins. Down below, the continuo hardly moves at all; the overall effect is quite grand, like a camera pulling back after a close-up. By avoiding a strong feeling of key, furthermore, Bach greatly amplifies the effect of a cool, misty evening falling at the end of day like no other.

As is always the case, Henrici's lyrics for the final aria are both shorter and more straightforward than those of the introduction. "Make yourself clean, my heart, I will myself entomb Jesus, for he shall henceforth in me, forever and ever, take his sweet rest. World, be gone! Let Jesus in." For the third time in the *St. Matthew Passion*, Bach uses the pastoral 12/8 beat, the previous two instances being "Kommt, ihr Töchter," the monumental chorus that opened the work, and "Erbarme dich," the grand aria of contrition roughly midway through the oratorio. Bach employs the rhythm (at least in part) for its feeling of vastness in "Kommt, ihr Töchter;" and in "Erbarme dich" it acts as a tightly woven rhythmic cradle for the intimate devotional sentiments of the text. Here, close to the oratorio's end, he uses the pastorale in its most traditionally rustic way, for its skipping, dance-like feel, with naïve associations of piping shepherds and bleating sheep in the oboes' trills, though they are not mentioned in the text). The melting warmth of its sound and feeling here are much like the famous chorale known as "Jesu, Joy of Man's Desiring" in the cantata *Herz und Mund und Tat und Leben*, and the lyrics are similar as well. In using this rhythm one last time in the *St. Matthew Passion*, Bach seems to be saying that the soul who has truly taken Jesus into his heart is no longer lost.

The instrumental group for this beautiful aria consists of two oboi da caccia, two violins, a viola, and continuo. The feeling of the sound is plainer, rougher even, than the delicate sonic veil of "Erbarme dich." The movement skips along happily, but the melody has a heartfelt sincerity that is unmistakable. This big-boned aria is built in three broad sections, with the middle moving into the minor key, but the range of emotions it expresses—its complex affect—combines unsullied joy and genuine gratitude.

The next sequence of recitative and *turba* chorus, covering Matthew 27:59–66 relates the burial of Jesus and events relating to it. It also concludes the narrative portion of the *St. Matthew Passion*. The section opens with the Evangelist relating how Joseph of Arimathea "wrapped it [Jesus's body] in a clean linen cloth, and laid it in his own new tomb, which he had hewn out in the rock: and he rolled a great stone to the door of the sepulcher, and departed" (27:59–60). Mary Magdalene and "the other Mary" sit, mourning, outside. Worried that Jesus's disciples will steal his body to make the Savior's prophecy of his own resurrection appear to be fulfilled, the Pharisees go to Pilate, asking the governor to set a guard outside the tomb. Bach sets this long, verbally complex text in a brilliant turba, which like several before opens with a dancelike section, then moves to a contrapuntal part, where every word remains clear. In a brief recitative, Pilate dismissively grants them a guard: "Ye have a watch: go your way, make it as sure as ye can." The tomb is sealed and the watch posted; and the drama of Jesus's crucifixion is over.

There remains, of course, the huge choral movement, "Wir setzen uns mit Tränen nieder" (We sit down in tears), which ends the oratorio. But the spaciousness and grandeur of Bach's conception for the work as a whole call for another movement between the end of the drama and the final chorus, which creates a transition of mood, from narrative back to reflective, and of sound, from the free mix of solo recitative and turba chorus to the richer sonority of the full double ensembles. Bach also felt the need for the soloists, who represent mankind as individuals, to sing their "personal" farewells to Jesus, before the final choral salute. Composer and librettist filled these needs with a complex dialogue for the four solo singers and the second chorus, accompanied instrumentally by the violins, violas, and continuo of the first orchestra and the full second orchestra.

Called "recitative" in the score, the structure of this movement is singular in the *St. Matthew Passion*, consisting of four different verses sung by the soloists, to which the chorus replies each time "My Jesus, good night." The bass opens the movement, singing "Now the Lord is brought to rest." For him, as for the other three, the strings hold the background with rich chords, silken yet strong. Over a mellow, rocking orchestral accompaniment, the chorus sings its sweet lullaby. The tenor enters, singing in tones that seem somewhat more agitated, "The toil is done which our sins made for him." But again, the chorus sings its calm reply. The alto's line, "O blessed limbs, see how I weep for you with penance and remorse, that my fall brought you into such distress," is filled with sorrow, as Bach shifts into minor key, remaining there for the choral reply as well. The soprano has the last word: "Take, while life lasts, a thousand thanks for your Passion, that you prized my soul's good so dearly." Her tone is fervent and awestruck. The chorus sings its final verse in the minor key, as this marvelously imaginative and expressive movement droops to its end.

The final chorus, "Wir setzen uns mit Tränen nieder" stands as the last of the three tremendous choral movements that are the landmarks in the work, and which are likely to be the first pieces the overwhelmed novice listener to the

St. Matthew Passion are likely to notice and remember with clarity. This gripping movement is of the scope and depth its crucial position warrants.

For this chorus Bach employs the form of the *tombeau*, meaning "tomb" or "tombstone" in French; indeed, French composers of the sixteenth and seventeenth centuries first developed the solemn dance movements so named as memorial works, often with the name of the late dedicatee in the title, perhaps the best known being "Le Tombeau de M. Blancrocher" by François Couperin. Musical memorials, of course, precede the tombeau; the "Déploration sur la Mort d'Ockeghem" by Josquin Desprez, composed at the end of the fifteenth century, is a profound tribute in music to a great composer by a greater one. The twentieth-century French composers Claude Debussy and Maurice Ravel took up the tombeau form, but in modern and ironic ways. Debussy's "Hommage à Rameau" from the first set of *Images* for piano (1905) is a lofty tribute in tombeau form dedicated to Bach's brilliant contemporary Jean-Philippe Rameau, and more broadly to French music of the Baroque. Ravel, in his 1917 piano masterwork *Le Tombeau de Couperin*, honors his great countryman, the composer mentioned in the title. None of the suite's six movements is itself a tombeau, but Ravel dedicates each to a different friend, all killed in World War I. Though in the form and style of the French *tombeaux*, the one with which Bach concludes the *St. Matthew Passion* exceeds them all in scope and intensity, which is as it should be, given the subject.

Bach had already used the tombeau form with mastery; the second to last movement of his *St. John Passion* of 1724 is a huge tombeau that takes longer to perform than the one in the *St. Matthew*. These two great laments have much in common; the main themes resemble one another, and Bach subjects both to painfully expressive harmonic treatments, going even further in the later work. But "Ruht wohl" (Rest well), the *St. John* chorus, seems the equal of its younger sibling.

Henrici's poetry for this grand closing movement is rich, but not so clotted with ideas and imagery that it interferes with the flow of the music. "We sit down in tears, and call to you in the tomb: rest softly," both choruses sing. "Rest, exhausted limbs, rest softly. Your grave and tombstone shall for the troubled conscience be a comfortable pillow, and the soul's place of rest. In highest bliss the eyes sleep there." Set in three broad sections, the chorus moves in a regal triple time, with the gravity of a cosmic dance. The sweeping arch of the opening melody is played by the full orchestral complements of strings and winds, echoed and extended sepulchrally by the tones of the continuo instruments. A sure source of gooseflesh and tears even to listeners who know it well, this mighty tune rings like a vast sigh, signaling unmistakably that the end of this tremendous drama has finally been reached. The melody's second part begins in a more hovering, temporizing mood also reminiscent of sighing, but ultimately moves toward its concluding cadence in an immense gesture of sorrowful grandeur. The first section of the chorus turns briefly to the major; and in the shorter, quieter middle section, Bach adds some detached notes for textural variety, just as he did in "Kommt, ihr Töchter." The return of the opening is a moment of terrible power and sorrow.

The second iteration of the theme ends on a crunching *appogiatura*, the grace note that Bach uses as one of the movement's chief expressive devices. Composers employ this added note, which inserts an approach of a half-step interval from above or below to a melodic phrase, in a variety of ways. Mozart used them often, generally to enhance the suavity of his melodic lines. But here, Bach systematically leans so heavily into the appoggiatura, creating a grinding dissonance at the end of this big melodic arch, that as "Wir setzen uns mit Tränen nieder" proceeds, the effect grows ever more jarring on the ear and nerves. The final cadence itself is on a drawn out appoggiatura that is especially painful. And Bach does not limit his insidious undermining of the movement's harmonic feeling to these: the entire chorus is full of restless chromatic alterations that make the music anything but calm and restful.

Bach probably had many reasons for doing this. One was surely his love of complexity; he rarely took the easy way; and his stupendous compositional technique was for him a source of pride. He would never write a simple harmonic accompaniment when a more complex, expressive one presented itself to him, as it always did. And of course Bach lavished all his technique and expressive skill on this, his most ambitious work. Another reason might have been to remind us that, while the Savior's sacrifice saved us, it entailed immense pain, physical and spiritual, for Jesus the man. The dissonances that spike the score of "Wir setzen uns mit Träiren nieder" thickly stand in the body of the music like the countless wounds in Jesus's flesh. The broken cadence created by the appoggiaturas, similarly seems a musical metaphor for Savior's broken body. Bach's dissonances express a fevered, nervous exhaustion that is remarkable, and possibly singular in his output; this, he seems to tell us, is the only way those who have witnessed the terrible drama of Christ's Passion *can* feel.

Modern, secular listeners also need to remember that the events of Good Friday and the days leading to it were entirely tragic to Bach's pious audience, as, indeed, they remain today. Triumph would only come with Christ's defeat of death in his resurrection on Easter Sunday, for which Bach and his ensemble would have performed one of his cantatas for that joyous holiday. In 1738, he adapted a secular cantata into the *Easter Oratorio*.[26] The sorry actions of everyone around Jesus, enemy and disciple alike, coming together and culminating in his death, prevent there being a tranquil ending to the *St. Matthew Passion*.

In "Wir setzen uns mit Tränen nieder," composer and librettist return to the Pietist conceits of "Kommt, ihr Töchter," the opening chorus. To round out the vast oratorio, the Faithful engage once more in a dialogue with the Daughters of Zion, sometimes singing together, at others calling antiphonally to one other. Bach achieves the sense of two groups calling and replying in several ways; as in "Kommt, ihr Töchter," he has the two groups alternate verses, and in this chorus he uses dynamics—loudness and softness—more extensively to create aural contrast and depth. The middle section of "Wir setzen uns" consists of the verses "Rest, exhausted limbs, rest softly," and "Your grave and tombstone shall for the unquiet conscience be a comfortable pillow," to both of which the second chorus replies, more softly, "Rest softly, rest well." The contrast between the more vigorous tones of the first choir against

---

26. Wolff, *Johann Sebastian Bach*, p. 284.

the more reflective, "weaker" sound of the second, is striking in its dramatic force, as though that group lacks the
strength to do anything but murmur the same grief-stricken
phrase over and over.

Like other composers of the age, Bach wrote instruc-
tions for dynamics only when creating an unusual effect.
The care with which he noted levels of loudness, softness,
and even shadings of volume in between in "Wir setzen
uns" is therefore of unusual interest. Novices will want to
pay attention to his alternation of loud, soft, and *pianissimo*
(very soft), and it is worth remembering and reflecting on
Bach's dynamic scheme, which consistently sets the hesitant
phrases, "Ruhe sanfte, sanfte ruhe" (Rest softly, softly rest)
at a lower volume, and the grand, arching phrase that concludes the big melody at *forte* (loud). "Schlummern da die
Augen ein" (The eyes slumber there), the phrase that ends
the middle section, is sung most softly of all. No description can substitute for listening; the sense and sensitivity of
Bach's approach to the text should make itself clear to most
listeners after a few hearings.

Like "Kommt, ihr Töchter" and "O Mensch, bewein'
dein' Sünde groß," the huge choruses that open and end part
I, "Wir setzen uns mit Tränen nieder" stands apart from the
Passion story. Each of these great movements serves its own
particular purpose in the structure—; "Kommt, ihr Töchter"
is a duly terrifying introduction to the terrible events to be
related; "O Mensch bewein," transplanted by Bach from
the *St. John Passion*, provides part I with a conclusion of the
weight and dimensions the composer realized were lacking
in his original version. "Wir setzen uns mit Tränen nieder"
acts not only as a structural counterweight for the two big

choruses in part I, framing the end of the *St. Matthew Passion* with a movement of comparable dimension to the others, especially the opening, but it also stands as a final word, a comment, like that of the choruses that close most of the classical Greek tragedies. Bach steps back in this final chorus from the events themselves, but these have been so shattering that the composer and musical dramatist conceives the movement in a tone of pain and grief, shot through with exhaustion, that is entirely its own. The last line of *Samson Agonistes*, Milton's biblical tragedy re-created in the form of classical drama, describes an enviable state, "calm of mind, all passion spent." But for the close of his musical dramatization of the Passion story, Bach provides no such comfort.

$\mathcal{N}$eglect, Revival, and Controversy
THE PASSION IN PERFORMANCE

THE *ST. MATTHEW PASSION* remained in a state of nearly suspended animation between Bach's death in 1750 and the revival of the work by Mendelssohn in 1829. The history of the work thereafter is remarkably interesting and colorful, the *Passion* being subject to changing musical fashion while becoming the object of ever-growing enthusiasm and reverence.

Bach's music was out of fashion when he died; certainly the idea of composers of the first generation or two immediately afterward, including his sons, writing in a style so saturated in counterpoint as Bach's is unthinkable; nothing ever seems less fashionable than a style that has just passed. In the decades following his death, the careers of Bach's successors at St. Thomas Church in Leipzig would certainly have been furthered very little by frequent performance of the late cantor's church music, which was complex, difficult and old fashioned. Of course occasional performances probably occurred as subsequent Leipzig music directors found themselves strapped now and then for a Sunday cantata, as even Bach himself sometimes was.

The complaint raised against Bach in his own lifetime, that his music was needlessly complicated and lacked warmth, continued to be raised in the late eighteenth century. One Johann Reichardt wrote this of Bach in 1782:

> Had Bach possessed the high integrity and deep expressive feeling that inspired Handel, he would have been much greater even than Handel, but as it is, he was only more painstaking and technically skillful.[27]

This view of Bach's music, so outrageous (especially in its charge that he lacked integrity) to modern music lovers for whom Bach is a godlike figure, beyond criticism—beyond praise—was apparently not uncommon when it was written.

The concept of a ruling affect—a dominant emotion for a given work—persisted, but for most composers, the new monophonic style, stripped down and simplified, was the preferred one. In this type of writing, broad, expressive melody sings above a variety of types of accompaniment that were artful but decidedly subordinate. The equal treatment of Bach's part writing was, for a time, gone. The music of C. P. E. Bach and Haydn from the *Sturm und Drang* of the 1770s displays a raw emotionalism and willingness to shock to which the strong melodic structures of monophony adapt well. The feelings expressed openly by Emanuel Bach in his music, while genuinely moving, are different in kind from the intellectual rigor of his father's methods. It seems safe to assume, however, that neither father nor son would have

---

27. Quoted in Steven Ledbetter, "The *St. Matthew Passion*."

expected the other to work in a different style from that which prevailed their respective day.

The belief, that Bach's music was utterly ignored for three-quarters of a century, however, is incorrect. No German or Austrian musician of the mid-eighteenth century grew up without studying whatever of Bach's was available locally, particularly the *Well-Tempered Clavier*. None of the alert and serious ones could ignore the old style, whether in fashion or not, for its shocking power in the hands of a master, and all strove to mine counterpoint for the tremendous expressive potential of which Bach had so convincingly demonstrated it was capable. Any well-trained professional musician can write a canon or a fugue; what has fascinated and stirred the best is how is how a master like Bach could make strict, even dry forms like these speak and sing with passion.

Thus, three of Haydn's six early string quartets, op. 20 (1772) conclude with brilliant fugal movements. These early works, while splendid, betray perhaps a slight self-consciousness, but the extraordinary Quartet in F-sharp minor of 1788, op. 50, no. 4, shows how far Haydn's mastery of polyphony had come. The opening movement, so obviously an inspiration and guide to Beethoven, is drenched in counterpoint, and the very beautiful fugue-finale looks back to Bach; nevertheless the whole piece could have come from no pen but Haydn's. Here the counterpoint is terse and terrifying in its Bachian intensity, while expressing the pathos-laden "pathetic" affect popular in the classical age.

Mozart, always on the lookout for fresh ideas, found himself repeatedly shaken to the core by his encounters with Bach's music. Visiting Leipzig in 1789, Mozart heard one of Bach's eight-voice motets sung by the boys' choir of

St. Thomas Church where Bach had worked, showing that Bach's church music was still performed in Leipzig. The story of Mozart's reaction is unverified but so lovely that one must hope it is true. "Here *at last* is something one can learn from," the composer who knew everything musical supposedly said, asking afterward to have the parts spread out so he could look at the music in score. Mozart was given a copy of the motet to take with him.

The intensive study of Bach throughout his career was productive for Mozart, who also admired and studied Handel's works. Usually the brilliant Austrian would then embark on bursts of fugue writing to develop his contrapuntal skills; the catalog of his works is studded with works in canon and fugue, including transcriptions for string trio of three fugues by J. S. Bach and three by Wilhelm Friedemann Bach. By the early 1780s, Mozart's mastery of the art was absolute. In the contrapuntal sophistication and expressivity of the first movements of the *Prague* symphony, and the Piano Concerto no. 25 in C major, and the finale of the *Jupiter* symphony, any listener can perceive the eruptive sympathy of Mozart's response to Bach. Counterpoint is always at or near the surface of the singular, sublime Divertimento for String Trio, K. 563 from 1788. Two of the fourth movement's variations are decked out in full contrapuntal style, the first a mysterious canonic section, followed by a chorale prelude that but for the instruments might almost have been lifted from a score of Bach's. "Der, welcher wandert dieser Straße voll Beschwerden" (He who wanders this street full of hardship), furthermore, the strange duet for two men in act 2 of *Die Zaueberflöte* is a fantasy on the chorale "Ach Gott, vom

Himmel sieh' darein" (Oh God, look down from heaven) by a powerful intellect that has reimagined Bach's style, not merely learned how to mimic it.

Beethoven, whose pun on Bach's name has been recalled, was brought up on the *Well-Tempered Clavier* by his teacher, Christian Gottlob Neefe. Neefe wrote self-servingly of his terrifying pupil in 1783:

> He plays the clavier very skillfully, with power, and (to put it in a nutshell) he plays the *Well-Tempered Clavier* of Sebastian Bach, which Herr Neefe put into his hands. Whoever knows this collection of preludes and fugues in all the keys, which might almost be called the *ne plus ultra* of our art, will know what this means.[28]

This amusing bit of promotional writing puts to rest the idea that Bach's music was neither played nor respected by the generation or two that followed. According to one astonishing legend, Beethoven could transpose at the keyboard every prelude and fugue of the *Well-Tempered Clavier* into any other key on request.

Throughout his career, Beethoven's compositions reflect the influence of Bach, from the Baroque feel of the powerfully affect-driven early works to the sufferings and ecstasies of the late piano sonatas and string quartets. Listeners associate much of Beethoven's imitative writing with the ferocious opening sections of the *Great Fugue*, op. 133, or the thorny counterpoint of the finale of the "Hammerklavier" sonata, op. 106, and the *Missa Solemnis*, op. 123. But the sublime fugues that conclude the Piano Sonata no. 31, op.

---

28. Cited in Harold C. Schonberg, *The Great Pianists*, p. 79.

110, or open the String Quartet no. 14, op. 131, are of a far gentler cast, and suavely expressive of the master's ecstatic and mystical soul states.

In the early nineteenth century, Bach's music may not have been performed a great deal in public, but it was a key part of the training of musicians, and his influence and reputation continued to grow in professional circles. In his seminal study *The Romantic Generation*, musicologist and pianist Charles Rosen demonstrates the profound and lasting impression Bach made on the musical styles of Frédéric Chopin and Robert Schumann, both born in 1810. These two giants, as far apart as any in temperament and aesthetics, both took Bach into their hands and souls, with their music blossoming as a result. Chopin, a daring and tough-minded avant-gardist, understood counterpoint deeply but published no fugues, though contrapuntal writing is common in his music. Two obvious and brilliant examples can be heard in the opening phrases of the Mazurka in C-sharp minor, op. 50, no. 3, and the gloomy canonic variation in the F-minor Ballade, op. 52, and there are many, many more. This brilliant compressor of material also learned from Bach and applied to his own music the integrity of each voice. He played from the *Well-Tempered Clavier* every day, claiming to practice only Bach for several weeks when preparing for public performances. When writing to pupils, he used *Travailler Bach*—"practice Bach"—instead of "sincerely" as his closing salutation.[29] Schumann, although more dreamy and emotional than the craftsmanlike Chopin, wrote his rhapsodical early masterpieces for piano carefully in parts,

29. Charles Rosen, *Critical Entertainments*, p. 29.

meaning that he accounted for every musical strand in a given work from start to finish, a discipline learned from his study of Bach.

Credit for the revival of the *St. Matthew Passion* goes to Felix Mendelssohn, contemporary and friend of both Chopin and Schumann. Grandson of the Jewish philosopher Moses Mendelssohn, this remarkably gifted and energetic musician was raised as a Lutheran by his parents, who had converted to Bach's own faith. A fine composer whose popularity is not what it once was, Mendelssohn would rank as an important figure for his revival of the Passion alone. The story of that revival—one of the most significant events in musical history—is remarkably interesting.

For Christmas in 1823, Mendelssohn's grandmother gave the fourteen-year-old genius a manuscript score of the *St. Matthew Passion*; there were still no printed editions of the work. Mendelssohn began to pick through the score and study it, presumably with mounting interest and excitement. By late 1827, he began to rehearse the work with others, still purely for the sake of discovery and wonder, without expecting to perform the music. Mendelssohn, who lived in Berlin, had been a member of the *Singakademie*, a prestigious choral group, first in 1820 as a boy alto, moving to the tenor section as his voice dropped in 1824. He also studied composition with Carl Friedrich Zelter, director of the *Singakademie* and an admirer of Bach's music, who had rehearsed with the group, but not performed in public, the B-minor Mass in 1811 and the *St. Matthew Passion* in 1815.

Thus, when Mendelssohn and his friend Edward Devrient, who was to sing the role of Jesus, approached Zelter in 1829 to propose a live performance of the work, they found a kindred spirit, worried about the outcome but sure of the value of the music itself. Mendelssohn himself prepared the performance score from which the individual parts were copied, and, at just twenty years old, assumed responsibility for the monumental job of directing a massive work that few knew and none had heard played in public; the *St. Matthew Passion* had not, of course, been heard since Bach's lifetime, quite possibly last in 1736.[30] Whether youthfully confident or simply crazy, Mendelssohn had to rely primarily on himself for this colossal project. (In 1826 Mendelssohn composed the Incidental Music to *A Midsummer Night's Dream*, considered by many his masterpiece, so his confidence in 1829 would have been well justified.)

According to Devrient, the excitement of the many participants grew exponentially as rehearsals progressed:

> All were amazed, not only at the architectonic grandeur of structure, but at the abundance of melody, its wealth of expression and passion, at its quaint and affecting declamation, and at its dramatic power. No one had ever suspected old Bach of this.[31]

The performance, which took place on March 11, 1829, itself stands as a landmark in musical—indeed, in cultural—history. But it was a performance listeners today would find peculiar. The chorus consisted of several hundred, with the *Singakademie* regulars in the first chorus and amateurs relegated to the second. (For reference and comparison, in conductor Philippe Herreweghe's 1999 recording, choruses 1 and 2 each have fifteen singers.) Mendelssohn cut the arias, which

---

30. Wolff, *Johann Sebastian Bach*, p. 295.
31. Ledbetter, "The *St. Matthew Passion*."

listeners now cherish as the jewels of the work, to emphasize the biblical text, and he placed the winds, of which only the transverse flutes resembled those of Bach's day, behind the other musicians, who filled three rooms. Another conductor was called on to keep these players together. Mendelssohn replaced Bach's wonderful oboi d'amore, which had fallen out of use, with clarinets, which had not become standard orchestral instruments until Mozart began to employ them regularly, around 1780, three decades after Bach's death.

The perspective that researchers of early music have provided for modern listeners make it easy for us to look condescendingly at the 1829 performances of the *St. Matthew Passion*, the first in about a century. For most modern listeners, the brisk tempi, crisp sound, and rhythmically alert playing by small ensembles of well trained instrumental and vocal specialists, make the idea of the sound of hundreds of chorus singers, lots of instrumental players, and a heavily cut score requiring two conductors unappealing, and even ludicrous. (Wilhelm Furtwängler's 1954 recording, shorn of seven arias and with massive orchestral and choral forces, might give some sense of Mendelssohn's performances.)

But it was then, at those three revival performances in 1829, that the early music movement began. Practical questions arose naturally from the process of preparing a work composed using what were lost instruments and practices. Mendelssohn began simply by acting in a manner that made sense to his intellect, which was formidable, but limited by ignorance of Baroque performance style. As time passed, people grew interested in hearing all of Bach's music, and the questions regarding how to play and sing it continued to multiply. One outgrowth of Mendelssohn's groundbreaking efforts was the establishment on the centenary of Bach's death in 1850 of the Bach-Gesellschaft (Bach Society), of which Schumann was one of the founders. Its purpose was the publication of Bach's music without editorial alteration, displaying the scholarly desire to rediscover the original sound and sense of Bach's music, which has continued and flourished in the original-instruments performances of the late twentieth century and afterward.

The existence of the manuscript score of the *St. Matthew Passion* given to Mendelssohn by his grandmother also suggests that there were others in circulation. It is therefore possible that the work was known, or known of, in some musical circles, if little understood. And in any case, it is clear that a revival of Bach's music was already underway in the European musical community by 1829, which Mendelssohn's efforts on behalf of the *St. Matthew Passion* brought into full bloom. His work was heroic, and his timing was perfect.

The first performance was so great a success that the work had to be repeated ten days later, again under Mendelssohn's direction, and once more on April 17 (Good Friday) under Zelter, since Mendelssohn had left Berlin. Other choral groups began to look into Bach's other works, and interest in his instrumental music swelled; the Bach revival was fairly underway.[32]

In 1899, nearly fifty years after its founding, the Bach-Gesellschaft completed its task of publishing what was at the time considered the master's "complete" works. But in terms of how the *St. Matthew Passion* sounded, it was another half-century until the birth of the period instrument movement

32. Ibid.

and the flowering of research into Baroque instruments and practices, when the kind of performances heard today began to dominate. There were a few exceptions; the great Wanda Landowska played on a huge customized harpsichord of a sort no performer today would dare use; the early-music orthodoxy would excommunicate her in no time. But so prodigious were her virtuosity and her communicative gifts that she convinced many a conservative to listen to Bach and other Baroque composers on a harpsichord. The more reserved American harpsichordist Ralph Kirkpatrick moved toward contemporary practice but also played Bach (and Scarlatti) with enormous intelligence, energy, and authority. In France, Nadia Boulanger discovered the glory of Monte-verdi's madrigals. But, as one commentator notes,

> The *Passion* was given complete for the first time in 1912 under Siegfried Ochs in Berlin—with 300 choristers and 70 strings. Still in 1950 Paul Hindemith felt obliged to denounce such casting. Even in 1979 Karl Richter chose the colossal tempi about which Albert Schweitzer had already warned in 1905. As a cult-work of middle class intellectuals the *Passion* had put on so much fat that an interpretation free of it became a real challenge.[33]

Orchestras had grown in size since the little ensembles of Bach's day; they contained, moreover, many new instruments Bach never used, including clarinets, trombones, and full percussion sections. Many of the instruments that remained (the horn being perhaps the most obvious example) had gone through changes in design so extensive that they bore

---

33. Volker Hagedorn, "Various Aspects of the Matthew Passion."

little resemblance to their Baroque forebears. String players, particularly violinists, employed a vibrato (the shaking in the tone) far more pronounced than those who performed in the first half of the eighteenth century. The sound of a great late-Romantic symphony orchestra is without doubt a wonderful thing, but it was inevitable that some musicians would begin to question whether that sound, which everyone always understood Bach could not have known, was distorting his music. Nikolaus Harnoncourt, the German early-music conductor who has recorded the *St. Matthew Passion* three times, aptly describes the sound this way in his notes to his 1970 recording: "The string orchestra will always spread a carpet of sound over everything; the delicate instrumentation . . . is swamped in the glorious, romantic string tone. We think we are hearing Brahms."[34] Big choruses also came under scrutiny as foreign to Bach's conception and experience. And, finally, as musicologists learned more about Baroque performance, the reverently slow tempos at which the *St. Matthew Passion* was performed began to yield to quicker renditions that immediately clarified the work's dramatic structure and flow. Bach always had to work with the instruments and players available which often may have been inadequate, but that fact does not justify substituting the Vienna Philharmonic for the carefully scored chamber orchestra of the *St. Matthew Passion*.

The twin revolutions wrought by the early music and original instrument movements are the subject of a major study beyond the scope of this short survey. But the trends away from big, supposedly all-purpose symphonic ensembles

---

34. Nikolaus Harnoncourt, *The Origin of the St. Matthew Passion*, p. 51.

toward smaller instrumental and choral groups and from slow, "churchy" tempos to more lively, dance-inflected speeds are clear and easily summarized. Today the field is held by the Baroque specialists; the last recording of the *St. Matthew Passion* by a major orchestra under a famous conductor was in 1972, with the Berlin Philharmonic under Herbert von Karajan. Even this recording stands as an oddity, apparently the last of its kind after the abridged English language version recorded a decade earlier by the New York Philharmonic under Leonard Bernstein. By the 1950s, more and more recorded performances were with reduced ensembles and, more commonly as time passed, original instruments or reproductions. Today's listener has many marvelous recorded performances to consider.

By the late 1950s and early 1960s, a number of good recordings of the *St. Matthew Passion* had been issued, including Karl Richter's first recorded performance with the Munich Bach Orchestra and Chorus of 1959, that of the excellent Danish conductor Mogens Wöldike leading the Vienna Chamber Choirs and the high-powered Chamber Orchestra of the Vienna State Opera, including some of the finest Viennese players of the day. Instruments specified by Bach, including oboi da caccia and d'amore, are in the recordings. (The fanatical care Bach lavished on his pointilist writing for oboes in this score can only be appreciated once the curtain of string sound is lifted.) Tempos were still slow by current standards; Richter's very powerful and moving version comes in at 3 hours 14 minutes, Wöldike's at 3 hours 19 minutes; Karl Münchinger's 1964 recording with the Stuttgart Chamber Orchestra is exactly the same duration. Most contemporary recordings run about 2 hours 45 minutes.

The chamber orchestras of this era are still bigger than the stripped-down ensembles of those employed in the last decade or so, but still offer a stylish approach to the music, and the instrumental textures are unquestionably clearer and more transparent. Vocal soloists are another matter; there is some old-fashioned singing on these, such as tenor Waldemar Kmentt's twentieth-century operatic approach to the meditative arias on the Wöldike performance. This is not to say that he is not good or touching—he is both—but Kmentt was an opera singer who specialized in the music of Richard Strauss. Listeners who know the *St. Matthew Passion* from post-1990 recordings that feature Baroque specialists, trained on the latest and best research about singing technique and practice in mid-eighteenth-century central Germany, may well be shocked by Kmentt's approach, which is broadly emotional and with a rich vibrato unknown in Bach's era. Nevertheless, his performance, and, indeed the Wöldike recording, have much to offer and are well worth hearing.

In addition to Karajan's 1972 recording, the best known of the old-fashioned recordings featuring large ensembles and famous conductors include a 1954 performance by Wilhelm Furtwängler and the Vienna Philharmonic, and Otto Klemperer's famous 1960–61 recording with the Philharmonia Orchestra and a glittering array of vocal soloists, which at an incredible 3 hours 44 minutes seems to be the slowest of all. There are still many enthusiasts who love these, but probably more who have come to view them as dinosaurs. Furtwängler's performance, like Mendelssohn's, is cut shockingly; many of the narrative passages in recitative are missing, as are seven of the arias, including the gems "Können Tränen meiner Wangen" and the stunning aria for alto with chorus sung while Jesus is on the cross, "Sehet, Jesus hat die Hand." The motivic accompagnato "Wiewohl mein Herz in Tränen schwimmt" (Though my heart swims in tears) is included, but not "Ich will dir mein Herze schenken," the aria it introduces. Furtwängler was a great conductor of Brahms, Bruckner, and Wagner, but his butchering of the *St. Matthew Passion* reveals his ignorance and fundamental lack of sympathy for Bach's aesthetic.

Tempos are sluggish; Furtwängler stretches "Erbarme dich," which runs a brisk 5:54 minutes in the superb 1996 recording led by Hermann Max, to a bloated, *ritardando*-laden 9:41 minutes. The difference between the old guard and the new wave is nowhere more noticeable than in the chorales; Furtwängler cuts these freely as well, but among those that remain he distends "Erkenne mich, mein Hüter" (Recognize me, my keeper) in part I to a grotesque 5:22 minutes; Leonhardt gets through it in 1:03 minutes, making it sound, with a moderate tempo and straightforward rhythmic integrity, like actual music rather than a watery soup with a vaguely religious harmonic flavor.

Klemperer seems more earnest in his insistence on performing the work without cuts, and even takes a run at arranging the twin orchestras and choruses in a way that allows the then-new stereo sound to reflect their separation. But his tempos are so slow as to give little sense of shape— let alone drama—to the work at all. The sound of the huge Philharmonia Choir is wooly, and the roster of solo singers, which includes the genuinely great operatic voices of Peter Pears, Dietrich Fischer-Dieskau, Christa Ludwig, Walter Berry, Nicolai Gedda, and Elisabeth Scwarzkopf, looks terrific on paper. But most of the singers themselves seem utterly lost amid music unfamiliar to them. Even Fischer-Dieskau and Berry, each of whom sang the work many times, cannot pull the performance out of the mud. Klemperer's monumental approach draws much of the music out to the point of incomprehensibility. Common sense would suggest that excessively slow tempos cannot help the *St. Matthew Passion*, which is already long, grave, and unbearably intense.

Like Furtwängler, Klemperer was magnificent as a leader of the music of many composers, including even Mozart and Beethoven, not to mention the high and late Romantics in whom both conductors specialized and excelled. Both were trained in a tradition that treated sacred choral works with reverence, emphasizing their prayerful over their dramatic sides. This meant big forces, and "reverent"—meaning very slow—tempos. William Mann's notes, written in 1962 for Klemperer's recording, while insightful in many ways, reflect the conservative view. First, while discussing the length of the Good Friday service, Mann notes that "Bach's setting lasts about three and a half hours," true only for Klemperer's rendition, which, as noted, is the longest on record. Fully aware of the shifting ground, Mann concedes that "We know that musicians in the 1960s make music in ways altogether different from their eighteenth-century colleagues." He cites several examples of instrument construction and sound, as well as vocal practice, that have changed, then concludes his essay:

> We cannot hope, and would not want, to perform the *St. Matthew Passion* as the Leipzigers of 1729 heard it; we can only try to make the music sound as nearly as we

are able, after careful study and thought, like what we believe Bach would have wished.[35]

Thus, in his *apologia* for Klemperer's approach, traditional except in its completeness, Mann suggests that Bach would have used a symphony orchestra and big chorus had they been available to him, which, while possible, is irrelevant. Just beneath the surface of these words rests the evolutionary assumption that the late-Romantic symphony orchestra is an improvement over Bach's chamber orchestras. Mann suggests that "we" would or should have no interest in how it sounded in 1729, believed at the time to be the year of its first performance. This argument is even weaker than the previous in at least two ways: first, Mann implies that no sensible listener of 1962 could be interested in a performance that by necessity sounded far different from Klemperer's, and second, he rejects the idea that the 1729 performance, with small forces but led by the composer himself, could be of interest.

Performances anchored in nineteenth century practice like these and Karajan's can be difficult for listeners who have heard more recent versions, or even for many enthusiasts raised on the old style but who know the newer ones, too. The difficulty is perhaps analogous to that of a wine lover who cuts his teeth on big, chunky Australians before curiosity leads him to the wines of France, Italy, and Spain—lighter, drier, lower in alcohol, and altogether finer; it is hard to go back once accustomed to the more delicate, drinkable styles of the Europeans. Even though there is some adjustment in hearing the smaller ensembles, vibrato-free

---

35. Mann, "Bach's *St. Matthew Passion*: The Passion Story in Music."

playing and singing, and quicker tempi, the gains in clarity and comprehensibility quickly make up for the apparent loss of gravity. What seemed sprawling and formless suddenly assumes shape, and even takes motion as musical drama; one even learns that a smaller ensemble moving at a faster tempo, can be just as serious, just as potent as the Philharmonia Orchestra and Chorus. And instead of being a solemn masterpiece listened to periodically out of dreary duty, the *St. Matthew Passion* turns into a fascinating, daring, passionate work of art, studded with an ever-growing roster of memorable moments to admire and love. (The original-instrument rule probably applies to all Bach's music, save for solo instruments, particularly the keyboard. His music works as well on the piano as the harpsichord, as long as it is played with clarity and passion, and pianists are not about to give up playing Bach.)

Of course the twinned early music and original instrument movements created some controversy; in the 1960s and 1970s the influential German-born philosopher and musicologist Theodor Adorno took an interesting swipe at the nascent fields. He derided these musicians as "Philistines, whose sole desire is to neutralize art since they lack the capacity to comprehend it. . . . [They] seem to wait with potential fury lest any more humane impulse becomes audible in the rendition."[36] A prolific and respected thinker and writer, Adorno dressed up his fogyism with greater skill than many who missed the old, rich sound, objecting instead to the leaner, "thin" textures and the supposed trivializing of the *St. Matthew Passion*, to them a liturgical, rather than

---

36. Quoted in Uri Golomb, "Modernism, Rhetoric, and (De-)Personalization in the Early Music Movement."

a dramatic, score that demanded a certain type of solemnity in performance. It was probably more a simple dislike of the new that motivated Adorno; the music suddenly sounded different from the way he knew it, and he was better equipped than most to unload a few high-toned objections.

Adorno had, however, put his finger on a dogmatic rigidity among the early music and original instrument scholars and practitioners. This tendency, common to purists and would-be purists, has spawned many bitter disputes within the fold on matters as broad as whether to use female singers down to hairsplitting over details of ornamentation. One such question, indeed, revolves around the fact that Bach did not use female singers, who were forbidden to perform in the Lutheran churches, presumably because they reeked of theatrical performers' low morals. All the choristers were boys and men, with the great solo arias for soprano and alto presumably taken by the most talented boys in their respective vocal classes. The first of Nikolaus Harnoncourt's three recordings employs only male singers; as does that of Gustav Leonhardt in 1990. But in both his second and third versions (from 2001 and 2007), Harnoncourt employs men and women. For the strictest purist, "How did Bach hear it?" is ever the standard. For such a person, Harnoncourt will have fallen from the way of true orthodoxy. Yet performances on disc led by John Eliot Gardiner and Philippe Herreweghe, all justifiably well regarded (Herreweghe has recorded the *Passion* twice), feature mixed soloists and choirs. Instead of female altos, however, countertenors sing the arias, bringing these versions closer to what Bach heard in his head and in the few performances he led. The point is obvious: even in "period" performances like these, widely appreciated as brilliant and satisfying, anything goes, as long as the artists can make it work.

The brilliant conductor, keyboardist, and all-around musician Joshua Rifkin, whose talents span popular and classical music, sparked one of the biggest and most interesting dust-ups within the early music movement around the *St. Matthew Passion* and Bach's other choral works. (It was Rifkin who suggested that the first performance of the *St. Matthew Passion* was in 1727 rather than 1729, a view now generally accepted.) Rifkin's shocking 1981 proposition was that Bach's chorus consisted of a single voice in each of the four vocal groups—soprano, alto, tenor, and bass—that made up his choirs. What this means, if correct, is that the textures and overall sound of Bach's choral works was far lighter and leaner than those employed by even the most radical of the early music conductors: four singers per chorus, eight for the double group, plus one high soprano for the choruses "Kommt ihr Töchter" and "O Mensch bewein." Herreweghe uses fifteen singers in each choir; Hermann Max a more typical sixteen, with both performing forces obviously doubled by chorus 2.

Disagreement with Rifkin was immediate and of a surprising vehemence. The audience of scholars who attended Rifkin's presentation of his thesis howled him down. An Internet search reveals at least one blog devoted exclusively to this dispute. Many who dispute Rifkin have cited Bach's famous 1730 memorandum to the Leipzig town council complaining of the inadequate resources he was given; others firmly believe Bach wanted four voices per section but regularly made do with two and three. Over the years, a number of well-known conductors who specialize in Baroque choral music have come around to Rifkin's point of view. These include the Britons Paul McCreesh and Andrew Parrott (who has written a book on the subject), and American Jeffrey Thomas.[37]

Rifkin has recorded a number of Bach's works, including the B-minor Mass, the *Magnificat*, and quite a few cantatas with a single singer per choral section. The results are striking in their lightness and clarity, though of course many listeners find them underweight. Rifkin himself has not recorded the *St. Matthew Passion*, but McCreesh's 2002 performance employs only nine singers in pursuit of Rifkin's theory, startling many listeners and probably infuriating more than a few with its lean vocal textures. The differences between what listeners are used to in the way of choral sonority and balance between vocal and instrumental forces are obviously great, but there is nothing eccentric or contrary about this quick, passionate, and eloquent performance. McCreesh's players and singers are brilliant, and the recording has been well received by the critical community. And, lest McCreesh be accused of dogmatism, his miniscule vocal force combines men and women.

Other well-regarded contemporary recordings of the *St. Matthew Passion* that combine up-to-the-minute musical scholarship with performances by gifted musicians include those led by Helmuth Rilling, Masaaki Suzuki, and Jos van Veldhoven. So durable is the work that, apart from the crucial decision whether to buy an old-fashioned performance or one using period instruments and performers who specialize in music of the Baroque era, it is difficult for the interested novice to go far wrong. For most listeners, the

---

37. Paul Griffiths, "Cutting the Bach Choir Down to Size."

quicker tempos employed in virtually all recent recordings will surely make this immense work more comprehensible as music and as drama. The fine versions from the transitional era of the 1950s and 1960s—Münchinger's, Richter's of 1959, and Wöldike's—slow by today's standards, but with much to offer, will reward those who know the work well already. Furtwängler, Klemperer, and Karajan are for those who desire a complete grasp of performance styles, stretching back toward the nineteenth century.

The history of the *St. Matthew Passion* is curious to consider. Bach himself led two performances that were fully documented (in 1727 and 1729), and possibly one or two others, but no more than that. Without doubt, it lay nearly dormant for close to a century, a difficult artifact of a lost age and style. Its revival in 1829, while one of the great events in musical history, was in a form far from what Bach composed. For the next hundred years, performances of a cut score at slow tempos by large orchestras and choruses were the rule. Even Karl Richter's 1959 recording, which was considered the last word in Bach playing and singing when released, sounds slow and a bit stodgy today, though still powerful, particularly in the choruses.

For its entire existence, from Bach's own struggles to shape the *St. Matthew Passion* into a form that satisfied him to present day feuds within the early music community over performance practice, the work has been subject to enormous shifts in form and fashion. Yet as much as any work of art, Bach's masterpiece fits the description, however subjective and trite, of *timeless*.

Selected Bibliography

Bach, Johann Sebastian. *Chorales, Book I*. Edited by Charles N. Boyd and Albert Riemenschneider. New York, G. Schirmer, 1939.

———. *Matthäus-Passion (St. Matthew Passion)*. Edited by Alfred Dürr. Kassel, Germany: Bärenreiter-Verlag; 1974, 11th printing, 2006.

———. *Matthäus-Passion (St. Matthew Passion)*. Edited by Siegfried Ochs. Vocal score by Kurt Soldan. Frankfurt: C.F. Peters, 1987.

———. *371 Harmonized Chorales and 69 Chorale Melodies with Figured Bass*. Edited by Albert Riemenschneider. New York, G. Schirmer, 1941. Distributed by Hal Leonard Publishing.

Basso, Alberto. "*The St. Matthew Passion*." Translated by Derek Yeld. Liner notes to *Matthäus-Passion* (Harmonia Mundi HMC 951676.78).

Geck, Martin. *Johann Sebastian Bach: Life and Work*. Translated by John Hargraves. Orlando, FL: Harcourt, 2006.

Golomb, Uri. "Modernism, Rhetoric, and (De-)Personalization in the Early Music Movement." Unpublished seminar paper, 1998.

Griffiths, Paul. "Cutting the Bach Choir Down to Size." *New York Times*, June 25, 2000.

Hagedorn, Volker. "Various Aspects of the Matthew Passion." Translated by Lionel Salter. Liner notes to *Matthäus-Passion* (Capriccio 60-046-2).

Harnoncourt, Nikolaus. "The Origin of the *St. Matthew Passion*." Liner notes to *Matthäus-Passion* (Teldec 8.35047).

Ledbetter, Steven. "The *St. Matthew Passion*." Academy of Ancient Music; *http://www.aam.co.uk/features/9908.htm*.

Mann, William. "Bach's *St. Matthew Passion*, the Passion Story in Music." Liner notes to *Matthäus-Passion* (EMI SLS.827).

Meier, Gudrun, translator. Program notes to *Bach Cantatas Vol. 7* (SDG 124).

Noss, John B. *Man's Religions*. 4th ed. London: Macmillan, 1969.

Rosen, Charles. *The Romantic Generation*. Cambridge, MA: Harvard University Press, 1995.

———. *Critical Entertainments*. Cambridge, MA: Harvard University Press, 2000.

Schonberg, Harold C. *The Great Pianists*. New York: Simon and Schuster, 1963. Reprinted New York: Fireside Books, 1987.

Schrade, Leo. *Bach: The Conflict between the Sacred and the Secular*. New York: Merlin Press, 1946.

Wolff, Christoph. *Johann Sebastian Bach: The Learned Musician*. New York: W. W. Norton, 2000.

———. *The New Grove Bach Family*. New York: W. W. Norton, 1980.